lonely planet

D0533822

BEST OF

Los Angeles

Sara Benson

How to use this book

Colour-Coding & Maps

Each chapter has a colour code along the banner at the top of the page which is also used for text and symbols on maps (eg all venues reviewed in the Highlights chapter are orange on the maps). The fold-out maps inside the front and back covers are numbered from 1 to 7. All sights and venues in the text have map references; eg, (6, C3) means Map 6, grid reference C3. See p96 for map symbols.

Prices

Multiple prices listed with reviews (eg [$10/5]) usually indicate adult/concession admission to a venue. Concession prices can include senior, student, member or coupon discounts. Meal cost and room rate categories are listed at the start of the Eating and Sleeping chapters, respectively.

Text Symbols

- ☎ telephone
- ✉ address
- 🖳 email/website address
- $ admission
- ☾ opening hours
- ⓘ information
- Ⓜ metro
- 🚍 bus
- Ⓟ parking available
- ♿ wheelchair access
- ✕ on site/nearby eatery
- ⛹ child-friendly venue
- Ⓥ good vegetarian selection

Best of Los Angeles
2nd edition – February 2006
First published – October 2002

Published by Lonely Planet Publications Pty Ltd
ABN 36 005 607 983

Australia	Head Office, Locked Bag 1, Footscray, Vic 3011
	☎ 03 8379 8000 fax 03 8379 8111
	🖳 talk2us@lonelyplanet.com.au
USA	150 Linden St, Oakland, CA 94607
	☎ 510 893 8555 toll free 800 275 8555
	fax 510 893 8572
	🖳 info@lonelyplanet.com
UK	72–82 Rosebery Avenue, London EC1R 4RW
	☎ 020 7841 9000 fax 020 7841 9001
	🖳 go@lonelyplanet.co.uk

This title was commissioned in Lonely Planet's Oakland office and produced by: **Commissioning Editor** Suki Gear **Coordinating Editor** Nigel Chin **Coordinating Cartographer** Hunor Csutoros **Layout Designer** Steven Cann **Cartographer** Anthony Phelan, Sarah Sloane **Managing Cartographer** Alison Lyall **Cover Designer** James Hardy **Project Manager** Rachel Imeson **Mapping Development** Paul Piaia **Desktop Publishing Support** Mark Germanchis **Thanks to** Emily K Wolman, Kate Evans, Carol Chandler, Darren O'Connell, Adriana Mammarella, Sally Darmody

Photographs by Lonely Planet Images and David Peevers except for the following: p9, p32 Lee Foster; p28 Cheyenne L. Rouse; p29, p35, p75 Richard Cummins; p64 Richard I'Anson; p80 Rick Gerharter. **Cover photograph** Star on the pavement of the Hollywood Walk of Fame, David Peevers/Lonely Planet Images. All images are copyright of the photographers unless otherwise indicated. Many of the images in this guide are available for licensing from Lonely Planet Images: www.lonelyplanetimages.com.

ISBN 1 74059 784 2

Printed through The Bookmaker International Ltd. Printed in China

Acknowledgements MTA metro rail system map © 2005 Metropolitan Transportation Authority

Contents

From the Publisher

THE AUTHOR
Sara Benson

After graduating with a liberal arts degree from university in Chicago, Sara jumped on a plane headed for the West Coast. A decade later, she's still living in the San Francisco Bay Area, and she'll defend LA to the death against any northern Californian prejudices. Already the author of several travel and nonfiction books, Sara wrote Lonely Planet's *Los Angeles Condensed* (the first edition of this book), *Las Vegas* and *Road Trip: Route 66*, and has contributed to LP's *California* guide. Her travel writing features in magazines and newspapers from coast to coast, including the *Los Angeles Times*, *Chicago Tribune* and *Miami Herald*.

Many thanks to Amy Lowe, Andrew Starbin, Andrea Schulte-Peevers and Jennye Garibaldi for helpful info. Thanks to editrix Suki Gear for being ace to collaborate with – again. Most of all, thanks to my family and Josh for loads of patience and support.

LONELY PLANET AUTHORS

Why is our travel information the best in the world? It's simple: our authors are independent, dedicated travellers. They don't research using just the Internet or phone, and they don't take freebies in exchange for positive coverage. They travel widely, to all the popular spots and off the beaten track. They personally visit thousands of hotels, restaurants, cafés, bars, galleries, palaces, museums and more – and they take pride in getting all the details right, and telling it how it is. For more, see the authors section on **www.lonelyplanet.com**.

PHOTOGRAPHER
David Peevers

David Peevers (www.peevers-la.com) is a photographer, writer and adventurer whose work has appeared in many Lonely Planet books and countless international publications and websites. He has been a white-water river guide, a blue-water sailor, a publisher of tribal Indian art and special-projects manager for the Los Angeles Business Journal. For nearly 20 years he has been passionately and professionally involved in promoting college education, winning many awards for his work. A citizen of the US and Ireland, he has lived in Los Angeles with his wife, Lonely Planet author Andrea Schulte-Peevers, since 1984 and is planning an imminent move to their favorite country, Spain.

SEND US YOUR FEEDBACK

We love to hear from travelers – your comments keep us on our toes and help make our books better. Our well-traveled team reads every word on what you loved or loathed about this book. Although we cannot reply individually to postal submissions, we always guarantee that your feedback goes straight to the appropriate authors, in time for the next edition – and the most useful submissions are rewarded with a free book. To send us your updates – and find out about Lonely Planet events, newsletters and travel news – visit our award-winning website: **www.lonelyplanet.com/feedback**.

Note: We may edit, reproduce and incorporate your comments in Lonely Planet products such as guidebooks, websites and digital products, so let us know if you don't want your comments reproduced or your name acknowledged. For a copy of our privacy policy visit **www.lonelyplanet.com/privacy**.

Introducing Los Angeles

Los Angeles (LA) wears its glamour like a second skin. A daily dose of California sunshine draws scores of gawking tourists, ambitious starlets, wanna-be rock stars and new immigrants each day. This is where the American Dream begins, and Route 66 ends at the Pacific Ocean.

The flags of three conquering nations – Spain, Mexico and the USA – have flown over the City of Angels. At its heart, LA is a fantastical hybrid animal. You can amble through a Mexican marketplace, learn the royal Hawaiian sport of surfing, feast on Asian fusion cuisine and be rejuvenated by a Euro-chic spa, all before the sun sets.

Often, things are not what they seem in LA. Even to call it a 'city' is an illusion, as it's really a collection of dozens of ethnic neighborhood and independent municipalities. Image is everything here. Hollywood, a name that conjures up visions of glittering stardom, is a broken-down district on the verge of urban revival. Still, when you bump into celebrities rushing out of a club on the Sunset Strip, or stroll the Hollywood Walk of Fame outside Grauman's Chinese Theatre, LA's movie-star magic works.

Don't take what naysayers tell you about Southern California (SoCal) too seriously. This megalopolis may chew up and spit out anyone who isn't quite A-list material, but you'll still feel like a star as you cruise down the Pacific Coast Hwy. Wherever you go, and no matter what you do, this sexy city of angels will have her wicked way with you tonight.

Not much room for the kids in this cruisin' machine

Neighborhoods

Los Angeles takes a chunk out of California's coast, bordered by the Pacific Ocean. Most of the city proper lies in the desert of the LA Basin, divided from the populous San Fernando Valley by the Santa Monica Mountains.

Metro LA's sprawling patchwork of vibrant neighborhoods takes time to understand. Decentralization is key, since LA County is composed of nearly 90 independent cities. Los Angeles is just one player, as are the smaller cities of Beverly Hills, Santa Monica and Pasadena.

The nerve center of several major freeways, **downtown LA** can be seedy, but it's also the city's historic, financial and cultural heart. Independent-minded travelers won't want to bypass its art and architecture. **Civic Center** towers nearby **Little Tokyo** and **El Pueblo de Los Angeles**, beyond which stands the dragon gate to **Chinatown**.

Get set for action on Sunset

A quick Metro Rail trip north-west puts you in **Hollywood**, no longer the abode of stars. Most TV and movie studios have long since fled north into the San Fernando Valley, especially to suburban **Burbank** and **Universal City**. East of Hollywood are the bohemian boroughs of **Silver Lake** and **Los Feliz**, bordering leafy **Griffith Park**.

West Hollywood encompasses Santa Monica Blvd, the epicenter of gay and lesbian LA, and the after-dark **Sunset Strip**. West of La Brea Ave, **Melrose Ave** has youthful street-level fashion designers, while upscale eateries, boutiques and art and design galleries are further west. To the south, the main draws of **Mid-City** are museums on Wilshire Blvd's 'Miracle Mile.'

Beyond the borders of rich-and-famous **Beverly Hills** and more refined **Bel Air** lies affluent **West LA**, where **Westwood** claims the University of California at Los Angeles (UCLA), while **Brentwood** boasts the hilltop Getty Center.

Santa Monica is the most tourist-friendly beach city. Next-door **Venice** is more funky, while ritzy **Malibu** lazes along the Pacific Coast

OFF THE BEATEN TRACK
Incognito stars chill out on Italian-flavored Larchmont Blvd (5, H4), between Beverly Blvd and 1st St. Travelers needing a break can lose themselves in LA's gorgeous parks and gardens (p25), or Bergamot Station's (p22) creative collection of art galleries.

Hwy (Hwy 1) northward. Among the South Bay beach towns near Los Angeles International Airport (LAX), **Manhattan Beach** is more chic than party-animal **Hermosa Beach**. Commercial **Long Beach** by LA's industrial port is at the southern end of the Metro Rail system, which extends all the way northeast to relaxing **Pasadena** in the San Gabriel Valley.

Itineraries

The charm of LA is that it's so easy to get to know. You may see more in just a couple of days (and nights) than most residents ever do. Relax: there's no need to get an early start, except at theme parks.

Freeways are as integral to LA life as sunshine and Mexican food, so consider renting a car unless you plan on sleeping, playing and doing biz all in the same couple of neighborhoods.

Beaches, many museums, TV-show tapings and celebrity sightings are all free thrills. Available at participating venues, the **Hollywood CityPass** (http://citypass.com; $49/35) includes admission to Universal Studios, some Hollywood Blvd attractions and a narrated city bus tour, saving you 40% off regular admission prices. The **SoCal CityPass** ($185/127) includes Disneyland Resort, Knott's Berry Farm, SeaWorld and the San Diego Zoo. Individual theme parks sell multi-day discount passes, especially online.

'Can't talk now, I'm...huff puff...blading!'

DAY ONE

Amble along Hollywood Blvd, then cruise past Beverly Hills, detouring to the Getty Center and winding up at Santa Monica Pier. After dark, hit the Sunset Strip or Hollywood's Cahuenga Corridor.

DAY TWO

Play all day at Universal Studios or head to Orange County's Disneyland. Join a TV-studio audience around dinnertime or catch a flick before midnight.

DAY THREE

Pay your respects to downtown LA. After lunch, shop in WeHo or bask in the sunshine on Venice's boardwalk. Unwind over cocktails at a star chef's eatery, then catch a late-night live-music or comedy show.

Highlights

DISNEYLAND RESORT (3, E4)

Having celebrated its 50th anniversary in 2005, Disneyland aggressively aims to be the 'happiest place on earth.' Carved out of the orange groves of rural Anaheim, in Orange County, it represents the pinnacle of a global, often controversial media corporation.

INFORMATION

- ☎ 714-781-4565
- 🖳 www.disneyland.com, www.disneytravel.com
- ✉ 1313 Harbor Blvd, Anaheim
- 💲 1-day single-park ticket $56/46, dual-park passes from $76/66; SoCal CityPass (p7)
- 🕙 10am-8pm, extended summer hr 8am-midnight
- ⓘ guided tours (☎ 714-781-4400; from $40), lockers, pet kennels, stroller rental & baby-care centers
- 🚗 25 miles southeast of downtown LA on I-5, exit Disneyland Dr
- 🚌 MTA 460 from downtown LA ($2.25, 1½hr), Coach USA (p83) from LAX, Starline Tours (p37)
- Ⓟ $10
- ♿ most attractions accessible; wheelchair rental available
- 🍴 Napa Rose (Grand Californian Hotel), Blue Bayou (New Orleans Square), Catal & Uva Bar (Downtown Disney); dining reservations ☎ 714-781-3463

Walt Disney first trotted out his cartoon mouse in 1928. He coined the phrase 'amusement park' in the '50s. Disneyland's opening day was a disaster, with 110°F-plus temperatures melting the asphalt pavement, but everything is now carefully 'imagineered.' Millions of visitors stream through the gates each year, mostly during summer or between Thanksgiving and New Year's. You could skim each of the resort's parks in a day, but it takes longer to experience everything, especially when lines are longest, on weekends and holidays.

You can avoid the ticket-window crush by buying tickets online or at Downtown Disney and then riding the monorail right into Disneyland. Once inside the park, the FastPass system at major attractions pre-assigns time slots for faster boarding. Note many rides have minimum age and height requirements. Bring a hat, sunscreen, snacks, refillable water bottles, and for cooler winter nights, dress in layers.

What amusement parks call 'rides,' Disneyland calls 'attractions.' A ride is a quick thrill, but an attraction is a journey into a narrative. Pay attention to the details you start to see as soon as you queue up. The real magic of Disney lies in its meticulously executed production values. Everything is impeccable, from the pastel sidewalks to the personal hygiene of the roughly 21,000 park employees, called 'cast members' in Disney-speak. But the resort is not

DON'T MISS

- an original R2-D2 from *Star Wars*, Tomorrowland
- live shows, parades & fireworks daily
- *Fantasmic!*, Frontierland's after-dark extravaganza
- Fantasyland's 'It's a Small World' animatronics
- *Aladdin* mini-musical at the Hyperion Theater, Hollywood Pictures Backlot

without shortcomings: the Disneyland of old had none of the product placement that exists here today.

You enter Disneyland theme park on **Main Street USA**, which cheerily re-creates Walt's hometown of Marceline, Missouri, c 1900. Have your picture taken with oversized Disney characters here or in tot-sized **Mickey's Toontown** at the northern end of the park. Lording it over Central Plaza is **Sleeping Beauty's Castle**, a pink confection inspired by Bavaria's royal palace of Neuschwanstein. Head to **Fantasyland** for rides inspired by Disney legends, while jungle-themed **Adventureland** has the thrilling Indiana Jones attraction. **New Orleans Square** is home to Pirates of the Caribbean and the Haunted Mansion. **Frontierland** has Big Thunder Mountain, a roller coaster through an Old West mining town. **Tomorrowland**, the park's retro high-tech showpiece, harbors Space Mountain, a screamingly fantastic roller coaster. A railroad loops around the park.

The resort's newer theme park, **Disney's California Adventure**, is a whitewashed version of the Golden State, but it's entertaining enough. Enter through **Sunshine Plaza**, presided over by a 50ft-high sun. Off to the left is the **Hollywood Pictures Backlot**, which boasts the Twilight Zone Tower of Terror.

Straight ahead is the heart of the park, **Golden State**. Here you can take a simulated hang-gliding flight over **Condor Flats**, get wet on the **Grizzly River Run** or get a taste of Napa at **Golden Vine Winery**. Everyone's fave 3D special-effects film, *It's Tough to be a Bug,* plays near **Bountiful Valley Farm**. A tribute to seaside resorts of yesteryear, **Paradise Pier** has a giant Ferris wheel and the California Screamin' roller coaster.

Between the theme parks, **Downtown Disney** pedestrian mall is jam-packed with high-concept eateries, shops and entertainment venues, including the interactive games at **ESPN Zone** and **House of Blues** (☎ 714-778-2583; www.hob.com) for live-music shows.

KNOTT'S BERRY FARM

Northwest of Anaheim, old-fashioned **Knott's Berry Farm** (3, E4; ☎ 714-220-5200; www.knotts.com; 8039 Beach Blvd, off I-5, Buena Park; $45/15-35; ⊗ 10am-6pm, extended seasonal hr; bus MTA 460; parking $9) was America's first theme park. While Mrs Knott fried up chicken dinners during the Depression, her husband crafted an Old Wild West ghost town to keep hungry diners amused. Every October, 'Halloween Haunt' antics run wild here. In Knott's California MarketPlace, you can still buy the famous fried chicken and boysenberry pie. Next door is Knott's **Soak City**, a summertime water park.

UNIVERSAL STUDIOS (6, B2)

Universal was founded by German immigrant Carl Laemmle in 1909 and moved to its current site – on a former chicken ranch – in 1915. To make a little money on the side, Laemmle sold eggs and invited the public to observe filmmaking firsthand.

The movie-based theme park is an entertaining mix of fairly tame – and sometimes dated – thrill rides and live action shows, plus a studio backlot tram tour. Universal is a working studio, though you're unlikely to see any stars.

The theme park sprawls across upper and lower sections. Among the rides, top billing goes to **Jurassic Park**, a float through a prehistoric jungle with a 'raptor-ous' end. The imaginative **Revenge of the Mummy** is an indoor roller-coaster romp. The sentimental favorite is **Back to the Future**, aboard a DeLorean.

Among the shows, **Terminator 2: 3D** combines live-action stunts with eye-popping digital imaging technology, seen also in **Shrek 4-D**. The movie may have bombed, but **Water World** has mind-boggling stunts. Audiences can join in unscripted **Fear Factor Live**.

No outside food or drink is allowed. Adjacent **Universal City Walk** is a strip of restaurants, shops, bars

INFORMATION

- ☎ 800-864-8377, VIP Experience reservations 818-622-5120
- 🖳 www.universalstudioshollywood .com, www.citywalkhollywood.com
- ✉ 100 Universal City Plaza, Universal City
- $ 1-day pass over/under 48in $53/43, front-of-the-line pass $100, Hollywood CityPass (p7)
- 🕒 10am-6pm, extended seasonal hr
- ℹ lockers, stroller rental, complimentary kennel service, Spanish-language tours
- 🚇 Red Line to Universal City, then free shuttle bus
- Ⓟ $10
- ♿ most attractions accessible; wheelchair rental available
- ✕ Daily Grill, Saddle Ranch Chop House (Universal City Walk); also p55

A crash course in movie-set making

and entertainment venues. Neon signs cast some Vegas-style glam.

Outside lies suburban **Burbank**, home to the entertainment industry since big-wigs started exiting Hollywood in droves decades ago. Further west is **Studio City**, with its nightlife and restaurant scene.

DON'T MISS

- free tickets to TV-show tapings from Audiences Unlimited (p27)
- concerts at **House of Blues** (☎ 818-622-4440; www.hob.com), Gibson Amphitheatre
- microbrews at Karl Strauss, Universal City Walk
- live music and Southern cookin' at **BB King's Blues Club** (☎ 818-622-5464), Universal City Walk
- bowling at Jillian's Hi Life Lanes, Universal City Walk

HOLLYWOOD (5)

Millions of dollars have been invested in rejuvenating legendary Hollywood Blvd. Even if it's still not glamorous, it's ready for a close-up now. Historic movie palaces bask in restored glory, it has some of LA's hottest bars and clubs, and even 'Oscar' has found a permanent home in glitzy Kodak Theatre.

Jimi Hendrix, Marilyn Monroe and Orson Welles are just a few of the celebrities being admired – and stepped on – day after day on the **Hollywood Walk of Fame**, which stretches along the boulevard from La Brea Ave to Vine St. Track the marble-and-bronze stars east to the **Hollywood Entertainment Museum** (p20). Catty-corner from the aristocratic **Hollywood Roosevelt Hotel** (p72) is **Grauman's Chinese Theatre** (p65), with its forecourt where movie stars have left imprints of body parts in concrete.

At **Hollywood & Highland** (p39), the Babylon Court frames perfect views of the Hollywood sign. Standing apart from tacky tourist traps, the **Hollywood Museum** (p20) inhabits a glorious art-deco building where make-up pioneer Max Factor once worked his magic on the stars. The **Egyptian Theatre** (p65) is Hollywood's oldest movie palace. Northeast on Vine St, the **Capitol Records Tower** (5, C1) mimics a stack of records.

INFORMATION

☎ 323-469-8311
🖥 www.hollywoodchamber.net
ℹ️ Hollywood Visitor Information
Center (p91)
Ⓜ Hollywood/Highland
🚌 DASH Hollywood
🅿️ Hollywood & Highland garage (5, B1;
4hr validated $2)
♿ most attractions accessible;
curbs dropped
✖️ p48

A little too much cosmetic surgery for this star

DON'T MISS

• public ceremonies on the Hollywood Walk of Fame (☎ 323-489-8311)
• interpretive history signs by Hollywood Blvd landmarks
• classic Musso & Frank Grill (p48)
• restored Cinerama Dome at ArcLight Cinemas (p65)
• outdoor concerts at the Hollywood Bowl (p66)

LA's fabled nightlife artery, the **Sunset Strip**, flows west on Sunset Blvd. **West Hollywood** (WeHo), an independent city that's the heart of gay and lesbian life (p64), is also flush with art and design galleries, as well as shops along famed **Melrose Ave**. East of the Hollywood Fwy (Hwy 101) are the bohemian-chic neighborhoods of **Los Feliz** and **Silver Lake**.

GRIFFITH PARK (6)

Just uphill from Hollywood, Griffith Park is a wilderness escape from LA's urban sprawl. Its thousands of acres make up the USA's largest municipal park.

INFORMATION

☎ 323-913-4688

🖳 www.cityofla.org/RAP/

💲 free

🕑 6am-10pm (hiking & bridle trails until sunset)

ℹ️ ranger station (4730 Crystal Springs Dr; 🕑 5:30am-10pm); free interpretive programs & nature hikes

🚌 MTA 96

🅿️ free

♿ some paved paths

🍴 outdoor kiosks & snack bars

On the slopes of Mt Hollywood, **Griffith Observatory** (6, D3; ☎ 323-664-1181; www.griffithobs.org) was the scene of James Dean's switchblade fight in *Rebel Without a Cause*. Its sweeping views are worth the trek, as are the public tours and planetarium sky shows.

In the park's northeastern corner are the **Los Angeles Zoo & Botanical Gardens** (p26) and **Museum of the American West** (p21). Railroad buffs love the **Travel Town Museum** (6, D1; ☎ 323-662-5874; admission free; 🕑 10am-4pm Mon-Fri, 10am-5pm Sat & Sun). It's not far from star-studded **Forest Lawn Memorial Park – Hollywood Hills** (p24).

Back near the southern entrance is **Griffith Park Southern Railroad** (6, E3; ☎ 323-664-6788; $2; 🕑 10am-4:30pm Mon-Fri, 10am-5pm Sat & Sun) and an outdoor swimming pool, **Plunge** (6, E3; summer only). For hiking maps of the park, visit the ranger station, nearby a 1926 **merry-go-round** (6, E2; ☎ 323-665-3051; $1.50; 🕑 11am-5pm Sat & Sun, daily in summer).

Scenes from *Batman* and countless other TV shows and films were shot near the wonderfully spooky (and artificial) **Bronson Caves** (6, D3), where a hiking trail offers good views of the Hollywood Sign.

Saddle up over at **Sunset Ranch** (6, C3; ☎ 323-469-5450; www.sunset ranchhollywood.com; 3400 N Beachwood Dr; per ½hr $35/20; 🕑 9am-5pm), which arranges popular sunset dinner rides.

THE HOLLYWOOD SIGN

Hollywood's, and indeed LA's, most recognizable landmark was built in 1923 as an advertising gimmick for a real estate development dubbed 'Hollywoodland.' Each sheet-metal letter is 45ft tall. Over the years, a number of pranks have been played, like when the sign was changed to read 'Hollyweed' after California relaxed its marijuana laws in 1976. It's now illegal to hike up to the sign. For good views, head to Hollywood & Highland (p39), Griffith Observatory or the Bronson Caves. Click to www.hollywoodsign .org for live webcams, a virtual tour and more recommended viewpoints.

BEVERLY HILLS (5)

The mere mention of Beverly Hills conjures images of fame and wealth. The reality is not so different from the myth. This is indeed where the money-ed set frolics. Opulent mansions flank manicured grounds on tree-shaded avenues, especially north of Sunset Blvd and in Bel Air. For a tour of stars' homes, see p32.

Affectionately known as the 'Pink Palace,' the swank **Beverly Hills Hotel** (p70) has served as unofficial hobnobbing headquarters of the power elite since 1912. Charlie Chaplin, Howard Hughes and Elizabeth Taylor are among the stars who've 'bungalowed' here. Featured on the cover of the Eagles' *Hotel California* album, the hotel had lost its luster by the 1980s, but it was revived by the Sultan of Brunei in the early '90s.

Rodeo Drive is where Prada, Gucci, Armani and Valentino trot out their glamorous fashions in sleek emporiums staffed by hotties as svelte as gazelles. It's pricey, pretentious and yet, somehow, oddly irresistible. Most people gravitate

INFORMATION

☎ 800-345-2210
🖳 www.beverlyhills.org
ℹ️ Beverly Hills Conference & Visitors Bureau (p91)
🚌 MTA 720; Beverly Hills Trolley (schedules ☎ 310-285-2438; tours $5/1;)
🅿️ 2hr free at municipal garages
♿ mostly dropped curbs & ramps
🍴 p51

Round up the brand names on Rodeo Drive

to cobblestone **Two Rodeo**, which has outdoor cafés with great people-watching and celeb-spotting potential.

That baroque Spanish Renaissance confection towering above Rodeo Dr is **City Hall** (6, B5; 455 N Rexford Dr). Its excess perfectly fits Beverly Hills, where the nouveau riche reach for the trappings of old money and European style. Around the grounds are artworks by Auguste Rodin, Isamu Noguchi and Claes Oldenburg. Nearby is the **Museum of Television & Radio** (p21).

Out west by 20th Century Fox's **Century City** (p39) complex, **Beverly Hills High School** (5, A6; 241 Moreno Dr) names Nicolas Cage, Angelina Jolie and Lenny Kravitz among its celebrity alumni.

GREYSTONE MANSION

Sweeping views can be yours at the hilltop Greystone Park with its 1928 Victorian-gothic **Greystone Mansion** (5, B3; ☎ 310-550-4654; 905 Loma Vista Dr; admission free; 🕙 10am-5pm), a wedding gift from oil tycoon Edward Doheny to his only son, Ned. The young honeymooners didn't remain happy long. On the night of February 16, 1929, Ned was shot by his male secretary in a ghastly murder-suicide. Scenes from *Ghostbusters*, *Witches of Eastwick* and other movies have since been filmed here. The mansion opens only for special events, but you're free to roam around or picnic on the macabre grounds.

GETTY CENTER (3, B2)

Triumphantly poised atop ridges of the Sepulveda Pass through the Santa Monica Mountains, the Getty Center campus unites the art collections assembled by billionaire oil magnate J Paul Getty with top-notch institutes focused on conservation, art research and education.

INFORMATION

- ☎ 310-440-7300
- 🖥 www.getty.edu
- ✉ 1200 Getty Center Dr, off I-405
- 💲 free; audioguide rental $3
- 🕑 10am-6pm Tue-Thu & Sun, 10am-9pm Fri & Sat
- ℹ strollers available; TTY ☎ 310-440-7305
- 🚌 MTA 761
- 🅿 $7
- ♿ excellent
- 🍴 The Cafe, The Garden Terrace, The Restaurant (reservations ☎ 310-440-6810)

Designed by Richard Meier, the acclaimed cluster of postmodernist edifices uses natural light and open spaces, recalling Bauhaus but with a result that's entirely LA. Stone portals frame 'the-city-as-artwork' views using travertine Italian marble taken from the same Roman quarry used for the Colosseum and St Peter's Basilica dome. Afternoon light draws with soft pastel palettes on the otherwise stark white marble that then seems to radiate. Around sunset, after all the school groups leave, is a serene time to visit.

From the parking garage, a driverless tram elevates visitors to a grand rotunda. Designed by Robert Irwin, seasonally changing outdoor gardens appeal to all senses. A zigzag path beside a stream, itself a sound sculpture using shaped boulders, echoes a medieval labyrinth, as do riotously colorful azaleas floating in the reflecting pool.

On view inside the museum's two-story gallery pavilions are samplings from the permanent collections and research library. Each year the foundation must spend millions to acquire new pieces, a quixotic directive direct from Getty himself, who was a notorious skinflint. Skylights shine upstairs on mostly pre-20th-century European paintings, while ground-floor galleries are given over to sculpture, decorative arts, illuminated manuscripts and photography. Interlocking pathways mean you may view the same works twice – but you'll never be bored.

DON'T MISS

- Van Gogh's *Irises*
- free garden & architectural tours, gallery talks & concerts
- Monet's *Haystacks*
- the cactus garden at South Promontory lookout
- Family Room hands-on activities & seasonal programs for kids

SANTA MONICA & VENICE (4)

Most visitors to Los Angeles ask first, 'Dude, where's the beach?' Chances are, they'll find it at the affluent seaside city of Santa Monica, with its miles of golden sand and paved recreational paths. The beaches can get very crowded, especially on weekends.

Palisades Park perches on a bluff overlooking the Pacific Ocean. To the south is the neon-lit arch over **Santa Monica Pier** (☎ 310-458-8900; www.santamonicapier.org), which boasts a vintage 1920s carousel that starred in *The Sting*.

Inland on the **Third Street Promenade** pedestrian mall, wacky street performers beguile shoppers, strollers and diners. A few blocks north is **Montana Ave**, a haute shopping strip. **Main Street** has hip boutiques, restaurants and bars running all the way south to Rose Ave, the border with **Venice Beach**. The namesake **Venice Canals** were opened to fanfare on July 4, 1905, by Abbot Kinney, after whom Venice's kinetic main drag, **Abbot Kinney Blvd**, is named.

Long a haven for bohemians, freaks and hippies, Venice's chief attraction is its mile-long **Ocean Front Walk**. Possibly LA's most beloved, zany beachfront, a paved shoreline path has separate lanes for cyclers and in-line skaters. Changing rooms and equipment-rental shops are strung out along

INFORMATION

- ☎ 800-544-5319
- ☾ beaches open until sunset
- ⓘ Santa Monica Visitor Center & Kiosk (p91)
- 🚌 Tide Shuttle & Big Blue Bus (p84)
- Ⓟ restricted/metered street parking, beach lots per day $6-10
- ♿ some dropped curbs, paved paths & ramps
- ✖ Santa Monica p52; Venice p53

Another California Governor candidate?

the beach down to yacht-filled **Marina del Rey**.

Galleries, studios and public art abound, much of it with a surreal bent. Gawk at Jonathan Borofsky's **Ballerina Clown** (4, A4; cnr Rose Ave & Main St) and Frank Gehry's **Chiat/Day Building** (4, A4; 340 N Main St), fronted by a huge pair of binoculars by Claes Oldenburg and Coosje van Bruggen.

DON'T MISS

- solar-powered Ferris wheel rides at Pacific Park (p30)
- bikini-clad bodybuilders at Muscle Beach
- Twilight Dance Series (p57) and free summer movies at Santa Monica Pier
- Camera Obscura (p29)
- Venice's murals (p22)

SOUTH BAY BEACHES (3)

Almost every beach along LA's south coast has a beautifully wide, sandy expanse. Water temperatures are tolerable by spring, peaking around 70°F during August and September. Most beaches are open dawn to dusk, when they are staffed by lifeguards (no *Baywatch* jokes!).

INFORMATION

- ☎ 310-379-8471 (beach conditions)
- ▣ http://beaches.co.la.ca.us,
  www.ci.manhattan-beach.ca.us,
  www.hermosabch.org
- ☯ beaches open until sunset
- ⓘ Long Beach Convention & Visitors
  Bureau (☎ 800-452-7829; www
  .visitlongbeach.com)
- ⊟ Pacific Coast Hwy (Hwy 1),
  south of LAX
- ⊟ MTA 439 to Manhattan,
  Hermosa & Redondo Beaches
- ◉ Blue Line to Transit Mall,
  Long Beach
- ⚓ AquaBus & AquaLink water taxis
  (Long Beach Transit; ☎ 562-591-2301;
  www.lbtransit.com)
- Ⓟ restricted/metered street parking,
  beach lots per day $6-10
- ♿ some dropped curbs,
  paved paths & ramps
- ✕ p54

Yuppies flock to **Manhattan Beach** (3, B4), where the surf music of the Beach Boys was born. Off busy Manhattan Beach Blvd is the pier, where you'll find the **Roundhouse Aquarium** (p31). At glam Raleigh Studios nearby, TV shows like *The OC* and *CSI: Miami* are shot.

In Spanish, the word *hermosa* means 'beautiful.' How appropriate for the buff, bronzed SoCal singles who hang at **Hermosa Beach** (3, C4). LA's beach-volleyball capital, Hermosa attracts a youthful crowd, thanks to raucous bars along the Pier Ave pedestrian mall. **The Strand**, an oceanfront paved path, connects the beaches.

A rocky precipice rising from the sea, **Palos Verdes** (3, B4) has largely unspoiled, rugged coastline with sublime views. A coastal drive takes you past **Point Vicente Interpretive Center** (3, B5; ☎ 310-377-5370; 31501 Palos Verdes Dr; $2/1; ☯ 10am-5pm), for whale-watching between December and April; **Point Vicente Lighthouse** (3, B5; ☎ 310-541-0334; 31550 Palos Verdes Dr; ☯ 10am-3pm 2nd Sat); and **Wayfarer's Chapel** (p24).

Across the Queensway Bridge from gritty downtown **Long Beach** (3, D4) and the **Aquarium of the Pacific** (p25) is the **RMS Queen Mary** (3, D5; ☎ 562-435-3511; www .queenmary.com; 1126 Queens Hwy; from $23/12-20; ☯ 10am-5pm Mon-Thu, 10am-6pm Fri-Sun), a grand dame among ocean liners. East of downtown you'll find the **Long Beach Museum of Art** (p20); the elite enclave of **Belmont Shore** (3, D5), along 2nd St; and the canal-laced borough of **Naples** (3, D5), for whimsical gondola rides (p37).

MALIBU & BEYOND (3)

Malibu is not a destination, it's a state of mind. With nearly 30 miles of coastline and more celebrities than anywhere else in LA, this is the SoCal dream realized.

Take your time getting here. Just south of where Sunset Blvd kisses the Pacific Ocean is family-friendly **Will Rogers State Beach** (3, B3). Driving north, off on a hilltop to your right is **Getty Villa** (3, B3; ☎ 310-440-7330; www.getty.edu; 17985 Hwy 1), a classical art museum reopening in late 2006. Seafood shacks stand by **Topanga State Beach** (3, A3), at the foot of Topanga Canyon Blvd, which climbs to the hippie-alternative community of **Topanga** (3, A2).

Stretched north along the Pacific Coast Hwy are the gated homes of Industry producers, directors and stars, and their private beaches. Downtown **Malibu Pier** has views of **Malibu Surfrider Beach** (3, A3), one of the world's great surfing spots. Just to the west is **Malibu Lagoon State Beach** (3, A3), where sea-spray blows upon **Adamson House** (☎ 310-456-8432; 23200 Hwy 1; tour $5/2; ☺ 11am-2pm Wed-Sat), a colorful 1930s Spanish-Moorish villa.

Gorgeous beaches offer coastal access up toward Ventura County. **Paradise Cove** (☎ 310-457-2503; 28128 Hwy 1; parking $25, 4hr restaurant validation $3) featured in *Beach Blanket Bingo*. Further north, off Westward Beach Rd, a trail ascends a coastal bluff to **Point Dume State Preserve**, where migrating whales can be seen from December to March. Beautiful, babe-a-licious **Zuma Beach County Park** has waves good for bodysurfing. Smaller gems include **El Matador**, **La Piedra** and **El Pescador** beaches. At **Leo Carrillo State Park**, a long strand of sand, surf and tide pools are yours to explore.

INFORMATION
- ☎ 310-457-9701 (beach conditions)
- 💻 www.ci.malibu.ca.us, www.malibu.org
- ☺ beaches open until sunset
- ℹ️ Malibu Chamber of Commerce (☎ 310-456-9025; 23805 Stuart Ranch Rd; ☺ 9am-5pm Mon-Fri)
- 🚌 Pacific Coast Hwy (Hwy 1) north of Santa Monica
- 🚇 MTA 434
- Ⓟ restricted/metered street parking, beach lots per day $6-10
- ♿ partial access to beaches & sights
- 🍴 p54

Families will love Will Rogers State Beach

DON'T MISS
- Self-Realization Fellowship Lake Shrine Temple (p29)
- Inn of the Seventh Ray (p54)
- movie-worthy drives along the winding Mulholland Hwy to Paramount Ranch (p26)
- Barbra Streisand's former estate, now the **Ramirez Canyon Park** (☎ 310-589-2850; www.lamountains.com; garden tour $35; ☺ by appointment only)

DOWNTOWN LA (7)

Incorrigible critics refuse to believe it, but the City of Angels does have a heart. In fact, few places in LA have as much to offer per square mile as down-town; it's rich in cultural history, architecture and the arts, and home to financial powerhouses and civic institutions, not to mention nonstop ethnic neighborhoods. True, many seedy streets are overwhelmed by urban blight (see p87 for personal safety advice). But don't skip down-town entirely. Come here to find out first-hand what 21st-century LA is all about.

INFORMATION

- ☎ 213-689-8822
- 🖳 www.lacvb.com
- ⏱ weekdays are the best time to visit
- ⓘ Los Angeles Convention and Visitors Bureau (LACVB; p91), roving uniformed 'Purple People Greeters'
- 🚌 DASH minibuses (p84)
- ⊙ Red, Blue & Gold Lines
- Ⓟ limited metered street parking, Chinatown lots per day from $3
- ♿ most curbs dropped
- ✖ p46

On the site where the city was founded in 1781 (p75) sits the free open-air museum of **El Pueblo de Los Angeles** (7, C4). The narrow, block-long passageway of touristy **Olvera St** has been an open-air Mexican marketplace since 1930. It has LA's oldest existing building, **Avila Adobe** (7, C4; ⏱ 10am-4pm), built in 1818 by a wealthy Mexican ranchero and one-time city mayor. The **visitors center** (☎ 213-628-1274; ⏱ 10am-3pm Mon-Sat) is inside the restored **Sepulveda House** (7, C4; 1887). Pick up a free **guided tour** (⏱ 10am, 11am & noon Tue-Sat) at the historic firehouse by the **Old Plaza** (7, C4). The best time to visit is during any of LA's many Latino festivals (p57).

The bite-sized **Chinese American Museum** (7, C4; ☎ 213-485-8567; www.camla.org; $3/2; ⏱ 10am-3pm Tue-Sun) is just around the corner from the plaza. A stone's throw north is LA's **Chinatown** (7, C3), with its vibrant pan-Asian community. During lunar New Year celebrations (usually held in February) a parade of giant dragons, decorated floats and lion dancers brightens Broadway, the main street. Kitschy **Gin Ling Way** has a whimsical wishing well, arty shops and hipster bars, with nouveau galleries on **Chung King Rd** further west.

East is **Union Station** (7, D4); built in 1939 as one of the last great US railway stations, it evinces Mission Revival and art-deco stylings.

Little Tokyo (7, C4) is lined with sushi bars, traditional Japanese sweet-shops and bonsai-sized gardens. During WWII, the community was hard-hit by the forced evacuations of Japanese American citizens to internment camps. Learn about it all at the **Japanese American National Museum** (p20).

LA's most important governmental buildings are in **Civic Center** (7, C4), distinguished most by the 1928 **City Hall** (7, C4), which served as the police station in *Dragnet*. A newer land-mark is the **Cathedral of Our Lady of the Angels** (p24).

Further to the west, a trio of theaters comprise the **Music Center of LA County** (7, B4), now joined by the astonishing **Walt Disney Concert Hall** (p23).

Southwest along Grand Ave is the acclaimed **Museum of Contemporary Art** (p21). At the southeastern corner of California Plaza, you will find **Angels Flight**, built in 1901 as 'the shortest railway in the world.'

DON'T MISS
• LA Conservancy tours & MONA neon cruises (p37)
• free **Grand Performances** (☎ 213-687-2159; www.grand performances.org) at California Plaza
• Olvera St's Xococafé (p62)
• free **Pershing Square summer concerts** (☎ 888-527-2757; www .laparks.org)

It closed in 2001 after an accident, but you can take the stairs down to Hill St for the **Grand Central Market** (p46) or continue south to the **Wells Fargo Center** (7, B4), with its little Old West **history museum** (☎ 213-253-7166; ☾ 9am-5pm Mon-Fri) and public art. Much of the financial district sits atop historic Bunker Hill, reached via the curvaceous **Bunker Hill Steps** (7, B4) opposite the **Central Library** (p23).

South of leafy **Pershing Square** (7, B5) are some of downtown's less savory areas. But the **Museum of Neon Art** (7, A5; MONA; ☎ 213-489-9918; www.neonmona.org; 501 W Olympic Blvd; $5/3.50, free 5-8pm 2nd Thu; ☾ 11am-5pm Wed-Sat, to 8pm 2nd Thu, noon-5pm Sun) is a bright spot.

On Figueroa St ('Fig' for short), die-hard sports fans stream into the **Staples Center** (7, A5). On the east side of downtown is the lively **Fashion District** (p40), a wholesale manufacturing center and discount shopping paradise, and SoCal's colorful **Flower Market** (7, B5; ☎ 213-627-2482; 766 Wall St; $1-2; ☾ 8am-noon Mon, Wed & Sun, 6am-noon Tue, Thu & Sat).

WHERE STARS ONCE SHINED
South of Pershing Square, on a down-at-heel stretch of Broadway, stand what remains of the early-20th-century movie 'palaces' into which Charlie Chaplin, Mary Pickford and Douglas Fairbanks once leapt from limousines to attend lavish premieres. Gems include the Tower Theater (7, B5), where the world's first 'talkie,' *The Jazz Singer,* premiered in 1927, and the restored Orpheum Theater (7, B5), a vintage vaudeville hall. Taking a weekend tour or attending a summer classic-movie screening with the LA Conservancy (p37) is just about your only chance to see inside these historic theaters nowadays.

Sights & Activities

MUSEUMS

Most museums are scattered around downtown, in Exposition Park further south, on Mid-City's 'Miracle Mile' along Wilshire Blvd, on Hollywood Blvd or in Pasadena to the north. For details on LA's kids' museums, see p30.

California African American Museum (3, C3)
This state-sponsored complex documents the historical African American experience of the US West. Galleries showcase traditional African art and works from the contemporary diaspora.
☎ 213-744-7432
🖳 www.caamuseum.org
✉ 600 State Dr, Exposition Park 💲 free 🕑 10am-4pm Wed-Sat, 11am-5pm 1st Sun
🚌 DASH F 🅿 $6 ♿ good

Hollywood Entertainment Museum (5, A1)
The history and mystery of movie-making are unmasked at this high-tech museum. Take a guided tour of original sets from *The X-Files* and *Star Trek*, plus authentic props and costumes.
☎ 323-465-7900 🖳 www.hollywoodmuseum.com

✉ 7021 Hollywood Blvd, Hollywood 💲 $12/5-10 🕑 11am-6pm Jun-Aug, 11am-6pm Thu-Tue Sep-May 🚇 Hollywood/Highland ♿ fair

Hollywood Museum (5, B1)
Survey a century's worth of memorabilia from a galaxy of movie stars. On display is Hannibal Lecter's jail cell from *The Silence of the Lambs* and sets from *Moulin Rouge* and *Gladiator*.
☎ 323-464-7776 🖳 www.thehollywoodmuseum.com
✉ 1660 N Highland Ave, Hollywood 💲 $15/12
🕑 10am-5pm Thu-Sun 🚇 Hollywood/Highland ♿ partial

Japanese American National Museum (7, C4)
Visually gripping galleries tell the story of Japanese emigration to, and life in, the USA during the past 130 years, including the nisei (second-generation) experience of WWII internment camps. There are Asian American art exhibits, too.
☎ 213-625-0414
🖳 www.janm.org
✉ 369 E 1st St, downtown LA 💲 $8/4-5, free 5-8pm Thu & all day 3rd Thu 🕑 10am-

5pm Tue-Sun, to 8pm Thu 🚌 DASH A, DD ♿ good

Long Beach Museum of Art (3, D5)
Ocean vistas are not the only beautiful views at this small museum, with exhibits drawn from California Modernism, contemporary and decorative American artisans, and early-20th-century Europe.
☎ 562-439-2119
🖳 www.lbma.org
✉ 2300 E Ocean Blvd, east of Cherry Ave, Long Beach 💲 $5/4, free 1st Fri
🕑 11am-5pm Tue-Sun, to 8pm Thu, extended summer hr 🚇 Transit Mall, then bus Passport A, D ♿ good

Los Angeles County Museum of Art (LACMA) (5, E5)
A staggering permanent collection of works donated by LA citizens and movie stars takes on a global outlook. Start at the multilevel Ahmanson Building. Across the courtyard, the Andersen Building displays provocative modern and contemporary works. Be sure you don't miss the translucent Japanese art pavilion, Hammer Building photography or

MAKING THE SCENE
Where's the hottest place for culture vultures on Friday nights? It may be free courtyard jazz (April to December) at LACMA (above), which also hosts Sunday evening chamber-music concerts in summer.

The UCLA Hammer Museum (opposite) has a sexy socialite's day-planner's worth of events, from poetry readings and conversations with film directors to heavy-hitting outdoor rock and blues concerts.

High in the Sepulveda Pass, **Skirball Cultural Center** (3, B2; ☎ 310-440-4500; 2701 N Sepulveda Blvd) puts on high-profile fine-arts performances, world-music concerts and films that pull in the cocktail crowd.

Latin American galleries at LACMA West.

☎ 323-857-6000 ⌨ www
.lacma.org ✉ 5905 Wilshire
Blvd, Mid-City $ $9/5, free
after 5pm & all day 2nd Tue
☺ noon-8pm Mon, Tue &
Thu, noon-9pm Fri, 11am-
8pm Sat & Sun
🚍 DASH Fairfax, MTA 720
Ⓟ $6 ♿ excellent

Museum of Contemporary Art (MOCA) (7, B4)

Architect Arata Isozaki built
this conglomeration of cubes,
pyramids and cylinders to
house renowned collections
of abstract expressionism,
pop art, minimalism and
photography, plus major
touring exhibitions. Tickets
may be valid same-day at
Little Tokyo's MOCA Geffen
Contemporary (7, C4).
MOCA's satellite gallery at
the Pacific Design Center
(p22) is always free.
☎ 213-626-6222 ⌨ www
.moca.org ✉ 250 S Grand
Ave, downtown LA $ $8/5,
free 5-8pm Thu ☺ 11am-
5pm Mon & Fri, 11am-8pm
Thu, 11am-6pm Sat & Sun
🚍 DASH B, DD ♿ excellent

Museum of Television & Radio (5, A5)

A West Coast counterpart of
the New York City museum,
it has an enormous archive of
breakthrough 20th-century
media. You can watch *The
Twilight Zone* pilot or listen
to the original *War of the
Worlds* broadcast at private
consoles. Assisted-listening
devices and closed caption-
ing are available.
☎ 310-786-1000 ⌨ www
.mtr.org ✉ 465 N Beverly
Dr, Beverly Hills $ $10/5-8
☺ noon-5pm Wed-Sun

Now put it back together again! Sculpture at MOCA.

🚍 MTA 720 Ⓟ 2hr
validated free ♿ good

Museum of the American West (6, E1)

Endowed by movie star and
singing cowboy Gene Autry,
it's a gold mine of Western
memorabilia, such as Annie
Oakley's pistols. In-depth historical exhibits test romantic
myths of the Old West.
☎ 323-667-2000 ⌨ www
.autry-museum.org ✉ 4700
Western Heritage Way,
Griffith Park $ $7.50/3-5,
free 4-8pm Thu ☺ 10am-
5pm Tues-Sun, to 8pm Thu
🚍 MTA 96 ♿ excellent

Pacific Asia Museum (1, C2)

Temple lions guard the Imperial Chinese–style treasure
house, a national historic
landmark built in1924 for art
collector Grace Nicholson.
Five millennia worth of art
and artifacts from Asia and
the Pacific Islands surround a
garden courtyard.
☎ 626-449-2742 ⌨ www
.pacificasiamuseum.org
✉ 46 N Los Robles Ave,
Pasadena $ $7/5, free 4th
Fri ☺ 10am-5pm Wed-Sun,
to 8pm Fri Ⓜ Memorial Park
♿ partial

Southwest Museum of the American Indian (3, D2)

LA's oldest museum has a
vast array of Native American
artifacts and art. Magnificent
highlights include Navajo
and Pueblo textiles and Hopi
kachina dolls, plus a prestigious basketry collection.
☎ 323-221-2164 ⌨ www
.southwestmuseum.org
✉ 234 Museum Dr, off
Marmion Way, Mt Washington
$ $7.50/3-5 ☺ 10am-5pm
Tue-Sun 🚍 I-110 exit N
Figueroa St Ⓜ Southwest
Museum ♿ partial

UCLA Hammer Museum (3, B2)

Known for its Honoré Daumier
lithographs satirizing 19th-
century French society, the
Hammer stages courageous
exhibitions by California
artists. Permanent galleries
spotlight impressionist and
postimpressionist paintings,
along with graphic arts.
☎ 310-443-7000 ⌨ www
.hammer.ucla.edu ✉ 10899
Wilshire Blvd, Westwood
$ $5/3, free Thu ☺ 11am-
7pm Tue-Sat, to 9pm Thu,
11am-5pm Sun 🚍 MTA 720
Ⓟ 3hr validated under-
ground garage $3 ♿ good

GALLERIES

To find out about upcoming art shows and gallery openings, check out SoCal's free monthly **ArtScene guide** (www.artscenecal.com). More galleries cluster on the Avenues of Art & Design arrayed around the Pacific Design Center (right) in West Hollywood.

Apex (5, F4)

An intriguing mix of 20th-century photojournalism and behind-the-scenes shots of the film industry, mostly in black-and-white, hang here. Visit the Fahey/Klein Gallery next door, which presents vintage and contemporary works in genres ranging from portraiture to landscapes, from Man Ray to Annie Leibovitz.

☎ 323-634-7887
🖳 www.apexfineart.com
✉ 152 N La Brea Ave, Mid-City 💲 free 🕥 11am-5pm Tue-Sat 🚌 MTA 212
♿ good

Bergamot Station (4, C2)

A nexus of the Los Angeles arts scene, this industrial complex harbors more than 30 galleries, studios and shops. Find offbeat niches like the Gallery of Functional Art, Track 16 Gallery and the Japanese paper shop. Saucy and irreverent exhibitions of new and experimental media hang inside the contemporary **Santa Monica Museum of Art** (☎ 310-586-6488; www.smmoa.org; $3/2).

🖳 www.bergamotstation .com ✉ 2525 Michigan Ave, Santa Monica 💲 free 🕥 most galleries & museums 11am-6pm Tue-Sat 🚗 off I-10 exit Cloverfield Blvd 🚌 BBB 7, 11 ♿ partial

Gemini GEL (5, D4)

This artists' printmaking workshop was founded in the 1960s and still thrives as a meeting place for New York and SoCal artists. Big names from the art world, including Jasper Johns, Roy Lichtenstein and Richard Serra, have crafted here.

☎ 323-651-0513
🖳 www.geminigel.com
✉ 8365 Melrose Ave, West Hollywood 💲 free
🕥 9am-5:30pm Mon-Fri
🚌 DASH Fairfax
♿ partial

LA Louver (4, A5)

Mere steps from the beach, a stark, minimalist barrier wall outside dramatizes the interior exhibitions of contemporary US and European art, including those by English-born pop artist David Hockney, now an LA denizen.

☎ 310-822-4955
🖳 www.lalouver.com
✉ 45 N Venice Blvd, Venice
💲 free 🕥 10am-6pm Tue-Sat 🚌 MTA 33, 333
♿ good

La Luz de Jesus (5, H5)

For a sneak peek at tomorrow's hot artists today, pop into Billy Shire's counterculture emporium. The 'Peggy Guggenheim of lowbrow' puts on shows of edgy, groundbreaking postpop works, including folk, religious and comic art. Shows change monthly.

☎ 800-978-7667
🖳 www.laluzdejesus.com
✉ 4633 Hollywood Blvd, Los Feliz 💲 free
🕥 11am-7pm Mon-Wed, 11am-9pm Thu-Sat, noon-6pm Sun 🚌 DASH Los Feliz
♿ fair

Pacific Design Center (5, C4)

A huge wholesale showpiece for more than 130 professional interior design showrooms, the Pacific Design Center, or 'Blue Whale,' as it is more affectionately known, allows the public to browse year-round. The MOCA (p21) maintains a freestanding exhibition space here as well.

☎ 310-657-0800 🖳 www .pacificdesigncenter.com
✉ 8687 Melrose Ave, West Hollywood 💲 free
🕥 9am-5pm Mon-Fri
🚌 MTA 705 🅿 $5
♿ excellent

MURAL MANIA

In North Hollywood, muralist Judith Baca oversaw the creation of the *Great Wall of Los Angeles* (3, C2; Coldwater Canyon Rd, btwn Oxnard St & Burbank Blvd), with its blazing images of LA's multicultural history.

More whimsical murals line Venice's Ocean Front Walk. Look for Rip Cronk's *Venice Reconstituted* (4, A4; 25 Windward Ave at Speedway) and *Homage to a Starry Knight* (4, A4; at Wavecrest Ave), a tribute to Van Gogh.

NOTABLE BUILDINGS

Don't miss Richard Meier's Getty Center (p14). For another look at LA's cutting-edge architectural scene, drop by the **A+D Design Museum** (☎ 213-381-5210; www.aplusd.org), which was moving at press time.

Central Library (7, B4)
A 1926 beaux arts triumph by architect Bertram Goodhue incorporates Egyptian and classical motifs into its artistic and architectural theme, 'The Light of Learning.' A 2nd-floor rotunda mural depicts California history. On-site art and photography galleries curate fascinating exhibits.
☎ 213-228-7000, events 213-228-7040
🖳 www.lapl.org/central
✉ 630 W 5th St, downtown LA 💲 free ⏰ 10am-8pm Mon-Thu, 10am-6pm Fri & Sat, 1-5pm Sun (guided tours 12:30pm Mon-Fri, 11am & 2pm Sat, 2pm Sun) 🚌 DASH A, B, C, DD, F ♿ good

Eames Office Gallery (4, A3)
Highlighting the life work of Charles and Ray Eames, both Mid-Century Modern architects and innovative furniture designers, the gallery sells replica textiles, interior designs, stationery and rare books. Staff can arrange self-guided exterior tours of the Eames House in Pacific Palisades.
☎ 310-396-5991 🖳 www.eamesoffice.com ✉ 2665 Main St, Santa Monica 💲 free ⏰ 11am-6pm Tue-Sat, 11am-5pm Sun 🚌 Tide Shuttle, BBB 1 ♿ partial

Gamble House (1, A2)
A defining masterpiece of the Arts & Crafts style, this masterful California bungalow was designed by Greene & Greene in 1908. Overhanging eaves and sleeping porches hint of Japan, while leaded folk-art glass blazes in the sunlight. Other notable Craftsman buildings are nearby on Grand Ave and Arroyo Tce; pick up a self-guided walking-tour pamphlet at the bookshop.
☎ 626-793-3334
🖳 www.gamblehouse.org
✉ 4 Westmoreland Pl, Pasadena 💲 $8/5; limited number of tickets available from 10am (11:30am Sun), advance reservations accepted for 2pm tour ⏰ guided 1hr tours noon-3pm Thu-Sun 🚌 MTA 267 ♿ ground fl only

Hollyhock House (5, G5)
Echoing Mayan temple designs, Frank Lloyd Wright's earliest LA project (1921) was a hilltop residence for oil heiress Aline Barnsdall, replete with favored hollyhock motifs. Some original Wright-designed furniture is in situ.
☎ 323-662-8139
🖳 www.hollyhockhouse.net
✉ Barnsdall Art Park, 4800 Hollywood Blvd, Los Feliz 💲 $5/3 ⏰ tours 12:30, 1:30, 2:30 & 3:30pm Wed-Sun 🚇 Vermont/Sunset ♿ good

Schindler House (5, D3)
Built by Rudolph Schindler (p82), this private house and studio was arguably

The Central Library – sshhh!

the birthplace of California Modernism. Guided weekend tours are led by docents from the on-site MAK Center for Art & Architecture.
☎ 323-651-1510
🖳 www.makcenter.org
✉ 835 N Kings Rd, West Hollywood 💲 $7/6, incl tour $17/16, free 4-6pm Fri ⏰ 11am-6pm Wed-Sun 🚌 DASH Fairfax ♿ partial

Walt Disney Concert Hall (7, B4)
A controversial Frank Gehry design, this silvery free-form sculpture of curving and billowing stainless-steel walls conjures visions of a ship adrift in a rough sea. The auditorium feels like the inside of a finely crafted instrument, clad in walls of warm Douglas fir. Self-guided tours don't allow entrance to the inner sanctum, home to the LA Philharmonic (p67).
☎ 323-850-2000
🖳 http://wdch.laphil.com
✉ 111 S Grand Ave, downtown LA 💲 audio-guide $10/8, 30min guided tours $10 🚌 DASH A, DD, F ♿ good

PLACES OF WORSHIP & CEMETERIES

Cathedral of Our Lady of the Angels (7, C4)

Spanish architect José Rafael Moneo has created a vast, contemporary structure without any right angles. Behind its austere mantle, monumentalism is tempered by milky windows and intricate tapestries.
☎ 213-680-5200 🖳 www .olacathedral.org ✉ 555 W Temple St, downtown LA 💲 free ⏰ 6:30am-7pm Mon-Fri, 9am-7pm Sat, 7am-7pm Sun (guided tours 1pm Mon-Fri) 🚌 DASH B

Forest Lawn Memorial Park – Glendale (6, F3)

Often cheekily called a 'country club for the dead,' here in grandiose surrounds over a quarter-million souls lie buried. Some crypts are kept under lock-and-key, like the Great Mausoleum where Clark Gable and Jean Harlow sleep eternally. Gracie Allen and George Burns are in the Freedom Mausoleum, while Walt Disney rests outside. Sightseeing is discouraged.
☎ 800-204-3131 🖳 www.forestlawn.com ✉ 1712 S Glendale Ave, off San Fernando Rd, Glendale 💲 free ⏰ 8am-5pm 🚌 MTA 90, 91 ♿ partial

Forest Lawn Memorial Park – Hollywood Hills (6, C1)

A catalog of dead celebrities – including Lucille Ball, Buster Keaton, Liberace and Gene Autry – rests eternally in a bizarre setting that combines

Norma Jeane's final resting place, Westwood Memorial Park

pathos, art and patriotism. It's just as hard to navigate as the Glendale branch (see left).
☎ 800-204-3131 🖳 www.forestlawn.com ✉ 6300 Forest Lawn Dr, Griffith Park 💲 free ⏰ 8am-5pm ♿ partial

Hollywood Forever Cemetery (5, H3)

An infinity symbol marks the gateway to the graves of hundreds of Hollywood legends, including director Cecil B DeMille. Rudolph Valentino lies in the Cathedral Mausoleum, while Jayne Mansfield has a lakeside cenotaph. Bugsy Siegel lies in the Jewish section, Beth Olam. **Cinespia** (www.cinespia.org) outdoor movie screenings happen in summer.
☎ 323-469-1181 🖳 www .hollywoodforever.com ✉ 6000 Santa Monica Blvd, Hollywood 💲 free, star maps $5 ⏰ grounds 8am-6pm 🚌 DASH Hollywood/Wilshire ♿ partial

Wayfarer's Chapel (3, C5)

Sitting on a knoll above sea cliffs, this glass chapel

(built in 1951) memorializes Emanuel Swedenborg, an 18th-century Christian mystic. Designed by Lloyd Wright (Frank's son), a colorless rose window above the chapel's altar perfectly frames spreading tree branches, elevating nature to religious art.
☎ 310-377-7919 🖳 www.wayfarerschapel .org ✉ 5755 Palos Verdes Dr, Rancho Palos Verdes 💲 free ⏰ 8am-5pm, Sun worship 10am 🚌 MTA 226 ♿ good

Westwood Memorial Park (3, B2)

Hidden behind a parking garage, this compact cemetery has the plots of many actresses who died tragically young. Look for Natalie Wood's headstone and the crypt of Marilyn Monroe next to one reserved for Playboy owner Hugh Hefner. Enter off Westwood Blvd.
☎ 310-474-1579 ✉ 1218 Glendon Ave, south of Wilshire Blvd, Westwood 💲 free ⏰ 8am-sunset 🚌 MTA 720 ♿ partial

PARKS, GARDENS & WILDLIFE

Don't overlook Griffith Park (p12) or the canal walks of Venice (p15).

Aquarium of the Pacific (3, D5)

More than a million gallons of water fill this happy, high-tech home for over 12,500 creatures from the bays and lagoons of Baja California, the icy northern Pacific, the Technicolor coral reefs of the tropics and the rich kelp forests found in local waters.
☎ 562-590-3100, tour reservations 562-951-1630 ⌨ www.aquariumofpacific .org ✉ 100 Aquarium Way, Long Beach $ $19/11, incl 1hr behind-the-scenes tour $30/23, incl 90min summer boat tour $38/28 ⏲ 9am-6pm 🚇 Transit Mall, then bus Passport C ⛴ AquaBus, AquaLink Ⓟ $6 ♿ excellent

Descanso Gardens (3, D2)

Detour northwest of Pasadena to these lovely gardens, with streams and a bird sanctuary. They're famous for over 30,000 camellias, which dazzle in January and February each year. Wildflowers and native plants burst forth in April, while roses bloom from May onward.
☎ 818-949-4200 ⌨ www .descanso.com ✉ 1418 Descanso Dr, La Cañada Flintridge $ $7/2-5, tram $3 ⏲ 9am-5pm 🚗 off I-210 exit Verdugo Blvd ♿ partial

Huntington Library, Art Collections & Botanical Gardens (3, D2)

Enter the rarefied estate of railroad tycoon and avid collector Henry Huntington. A 1910 beaux arts mansion houses British and French 18th-century paintings, while the library displays rare exquisite treasures such as a Gutenberg Bible and a double-elephant folio edition of Audubon's *Birds of America*. A stroll around the expansive botanical gardens is a feast for the senses, with 15,000 plant varieties in a dozen themed landscapes.
☎ 626-405-2100, tea room reservations 626-683-8131 ⌨ www.huntington.org ✉ 1151 Oxford Rd, San Marino $ $15/6-12, afternoon tea $15/7.50 ⏲ 10:30am-4:30pm Tue-Sun Jun-Aug, noon-4:30pm Tue-Fri, 10:30am-4:30pm Sat & Sun Sep-May 🚗 take Colorado Blvd E, then S Allen Ave ♿ all bldgs, most gardens

Los Angeles County Arboretum & Botanic Garden (3, E2)

It was once the private abode of Elias 'Lucky' Baldwin, one of LA's early real-estate tycoons. Much of John Huston's *The African Queen* (starring Humphrey Bogart and Katharine Hepburn) was filmed in this sprawling park.
☎ 626-821-3222 ⌨ www.arboretum.org ✉ 301 N Baldwin Ave, Arcadia $ $7/2.50-5, free 3rd Tue, tram $3 ⏲ 9am-5pm, tram 11am-3pm 🚌 MTA 268 ♿ some paths

20,000 kids under the sea, Aquarium of the Pacific

Los Angeles Zoo & Botanical Gardens (6, E1)

Starting out in 1912 as a refuge for retired circus animals, the LA Zoo has helped the California condor and countless other species inch their way back from extinction. The beloved elephant Gita and alligator Methuselah have resided here since day one.

☎ 323-644-4200 ⌨ www.lazoo.org ✉ 5333 Zoo Dr, Griffith Park $ $10/5-7, shuttle pass $4/2 ⏱ 10am-5pm Sep-Jun, 10am-6pm Jul & Aug 🚌 MTA 96 ♿ excellent

Mildred E Mathias Botanical Garden (3, B2)

In the southeast corner of the UCLA campus, this humble 7-acre haven has more than 5000 native and exotic plants and flowers. It's a quick escape for city dwellers and stressed-out students.

☎ 310-825-1260 ⌨ www .botgard.ucla.edu/bg-home .htm ✉ off Tiverton Ave, north of Wilshire Blvd, Westwood $ free ⏱ 8am-4pm 🚌 BBB 1, 2, 3 ♿ fair

Santa Anita Racetrack (3, E2)

Southern California's oldest and most prestigious thoroughbred racing track, at Santa Anita Park, is the home of the legendary Seabiscuit, the rags-to-riches horse whose inspiring story became a blockbuster movie. During race season, tram tours take you to Seabiscuit's barn, the jockeys' room and training areas.

☎ 626-574-7223, tour reservations 626-574-6677 ⌨ www.santaanita.com ✉ 285 W Huntington Dr, Arcadia $ tours free (reservations required), tickets $5-8.50 ⏱ Dec 26-late Apr & early Oct-early Nov, tours 8:30 & 9:45am Sat & Sun 🚌 MTA 79 🅿 $5 ♿ good

Santa Monica Mountains National Recreation Area (3, A2)

Chaparral grows in thickly forested canyons, while coastal beach dunes enjoy a Mediterranean climate. Hidden in this epic wilderness are **Malibu Creek State Park**, where *M*A*S*H* was filmed; the western-town film set at **Paramount Ranch**, off Mulholland Hwy; and the 60-mile **Backbone Trail**, connecting many smaller parks. Visit in spring or fall.

☎ 805-370-2301, shuttle info 888-734-2323 ⌨ www.nps.gov/samo ✉ btwn Pacific Coast Hwy (Hwy 1) & Ventura Fwy (Hwy 101) $ nominal entrance fees ⏱ most parks open sunrise-sunset 🚌 MTA 434 to Malibu, then ParkLINK shuttle ($1) ♿ some trails accessible

UCLA Hannah Carter Japanese Garden (3, B2)

Fortunately, there aren't many visitors at this peaceful hillside Kyoto-style garden, where 1000-year-old stone carvings, a teahouse and Japanese maples meld with perfect contemplation. A slender garden of Hawaiian plants lies off to one side.

☎ 310-794-0320 ⌨ www .japanesegarden.ucla.edu ✉ 10619 Bellagio Rd, Bel Air $ free ⏱ 10am-3pm Tues, Wed & Fri (reservations required) 🅿 limited free parking

Will Rogers State Historic Park (3, B2)

Hollywood cowboy and humorist Will Rogers traded his Beverly Hills mansion for this mountainous retreat, up until his death in an Alaskan plane crash in 1935. Spencer Tracy and Walt Disney played polo on the lawn, where matches are still held on weekends from April to October. Pet-friendly hiking trails lead up into the chaparral, including to Inspiration Point.

☎ 310-454-8212 ⌨ http://cal-parks.ca.gov ✉ off Sunset Blvd, Pacific Palisades $ free ⏱ 8am-sunset, ranch tours 11am, 1 & 2pm Tue-Sat 🚌 MTA 2 🅿 $7 ♿ partial

LEVIATHANS OF THE DEEP

When you tire of movie-star sightings, crane your neck seaward to watch migrating grey whales en route between the arctic Bering Sea and southern Baja between December and April. The best coastal observation spot is Point Vicente Interpretive Center (p16). Whale-watching excursion boats depart between January and March from Marina del Rey (3, B3), San Pedro (3, C5) and Long Beach (3, D4).

TV & MOVIE STUDIOS

The television production season runs from August to March. The audience rules for live tapings can be draconian (under-16s are not admitted, no one can arrive late or leave early etc). Movie and TV studios give tours year-round, but star sightings are not very likely, especially during the summer hiatus.

Audiences Unlimited (6, B2)
They handle tickets for the most coveted shows, like *That '70s Show* and *Will & Grace*. Often you can pick up same-day tickets from their booth at Universal Studios (p10). Advance tickets are available online up to 30 days beforehand.
☎ 818-753-3470
🖥 www.tvtickets.com
💲 free 🚌 some free shuttles from Universal Studios
♿ good

CBS Television City (5, E4)
To be a contestant on the kitschy *The Price is Right* game show, click for tickets online or stop by the CBS

ticket window at the corner of Fairfax Ave.
☎ 323-575-2458
🖥 www.cbs.com ✉ 7800 Beverly Blvd, Mid-City
💲 free 🕙 ticket window 9am-5pm Mon-Fri (from 7:30am some taping days)
🚌 DASH Fairfax ♿ good

NBC Studios (6, C1)
NBC has produced such legends as Johnny Carson and Jay Leno, plus a string of recent sitcom smashes. Tickets for *The Tonight Show* are available in-person starting at 8am, or by mail at least six weeks in advance. Studio tours drop by the set, with other stops at wardrobe or props.
☎ 818-840-3537
🖥 www.nbc.com ✉ 3000 W Alameda Ave, Burbank
💲 1hr tours $7.50/4
🕙 tours 9am-3pm Mon-Fri, also 10am-2pm Sat Jul & Aug, every half hr (no reservations)
🚌 MTA 96 ♿ fair

Sony Pictures Studios (3, C3)
Once the most powerful Hollywood studio, MGM had so many celebs under contract that its motto was 'More stars than there are in heaven.' MGM was gobbled up by Sony, which gives ho-hum

tours that visit the set of *Jeopardy!* or *Wheel of Fortune*. For free tickets to tapings, click to www.tvtix.com.
☎ 310-520-8687 🖥 www .sonypicturesstudios.com
✉ 10202 W Washington Blvd, Culver City 💲 2hr tours $25 (under-12s not admitted)
🕙 tours 9:30am-2:30pm Mon-Fri (reservations recommended) 🚌 MTA 33, 333
♿ fair

Warner Bros VIP Studio Tour (6, B1)
Unlike at Universal Studios (p10), the good ol' WB doesn't razzle-dazzle you with theme park rides, but gives you a realistic glimpse into the methodic madness of movie and TV show production. Comfy trams, smart tour guides, a museum of memorabilia and small groups make this the best studio tour.
☎ 818-977-8687
🖥 www.wbstudiotour.com
✉ 3400 Riverside Dr, Burbank 💲 2hr tours $39 (under-8s not admitted)
🕙 9am-3pm Mon-Fri Oct-Apr, until 4pm May-Sep, tours half-hourly (reservations accepted) 🚌 MTA 96
🅿 parking lot N (gate 6) $5
♿ good

The gates to fame and fortune await

SPAS & BEAUTY

Most day spas offer massage therapy, facials, manicures and pedicures, and waxing and tanning services. Both men and women are welcome, unless otherwise stated; advance appointments are required. If a service charge isn't included, remember to tip at least 10%.

Kinara (5, C4)

Ultra-fashionable Kinara offers 'red carpet' facials, hydrotherapy baths worthy of Cleopatra, Polynesian-style body scrubs and Swedish massage. Sofia Coppola and Christina Ricci shine here. Wholesome, organic spa cuisine is served at the café.
☎ 310-657-9188
🖳 www.kinaraspa.com
✉ 656 N Robertson Blvd, West Hollywood 💲 call for rates 🕒 9am-9pm Tue-Fri, 9am-8pm Sat, 10am-6pm Sun 🚍 MTA 220 ♿ fair

Miyako Hotel Health Spa (7, C4)

At this Little Tokyo hideaway, shiatsu massage (from $60) includes use of the sauna, Jacuzzis, fitness room and even an Internet-connected computer – what a bargain!
☎ 213-617-0004
🖳 www.miyakoinn.com

✉ 328 E 1st St, downtown LA 💲 day pass $25 🕒 noon-midnight (last entry 10pm) 🚍 DASH A, DD

Ole Henriksen Face & Body Shop (5, C3)

On the other side of the shoji-screened wall from you might be a celeb like Ashley Judd or Charlize Theron. Show up early for your signature facial to enjoy the eucalyptus steam room (bring a swimsuit). The Scandinavian owner also designed the treatments at ONE Spa at Santa Monica's Shutters on the Beach (p70).
☎ 310-854-7700
🖳 www.olefacebody.com
✉ 8622A W Sunset Blvd, West Hollywood 💲 most treatments $60-200
🕒 8am-5pm Mon, 8am-8pm Tue-Sat, 9:30am-4:30pm Sun 🚍 MTA 2 ♿ fair

Olympic Spa (5, H6)

This out-of-the-way women's bathhouse in Koreatown rejuvenates with its jade-tiled and mineral steam saunas, clay dry sauna, hot mugwort tea pool and hearty scrubs that will exfoliate you to a baby's smoothness.
☎ 323-857-0666
🖳 www.olympicspala.com
✉ 3915 W Olympic Blvd, Koreatown 💲 entry

Yoga-watch extra on an LA beach

$15, treatments from $30
🕒 9am-10pm 🚍 MTA 328

Ona Spa (5, F4)

Above a hair salon to the stars, this Balinese-styled retreat has all the perks you could wish for (the name means 'all things good'). After an all-organic body polish, facial and hot-stone couples' massage, relax with a serene pot of tea. Stars like Meg Ryan and Uma Thurman have been blessed by beauty here.
☎ 323-931-4442 🖳 www.onaspa.com ✉ 7373 Beverly Blvd, Mid-City 💲 call for rates 🕒 10am-8pm Tue-Sat, to 10pm Thu, 11am-7pm Sun 🚍 MTA 714

STRETCHING WITH THE STARS

Famous bods like Cindy Crawford's have followed yogi Gurmukh to kundalini-style yoga studio **Golden Bridge** (5, G3; ☎ 323-936-4172; 6322 De Longpre Ave, Hollywood), while **Mark Blanchard's Progressive Power Yoga** (6, A1; ☎ 818-769-6427; 4344 Tujunga Ave, Studio City) is less about finding inner peace than firming A-listers' abs. Core fusion fitness and even 'cardio striptease' all have made waves in LA, especially at sceney gyms favored by hunky and svelte stars, like Crunch Gym (p87).

QUIRKY LA

Camera Obscura (4, A2)
An early version of the single-lens reflex camera, this was quite the sensation when it opened in 1899. Ask for a key at the Senior Recreation Center, then head up the dark stairway to see the scientific magic.
☎ 310-458-8644
✉ 1450 Ocean Ave, Santa Monica ⑤ nominal fee
⏰ 9am-3pm Mon-Fri, 11am-3pm Sat & Sun
🚌 Tide Shuttle, BBB 1, 7, 10

Clifton's Cafeteria (7, B5)
This venerable eatery was started in 1931 by a Salvation Army captain who doled out free grub to starving Angelenos during the Great Depression. The ultra-campy setting – an enchanted forest with fake trees, squirrels and deer – makes it truly odd.
☎ 213-627-1673 ✉ 648 Broadway, downtown LA
⏰ 6:30am-7:30pm
🚌 DASH E ♿ good

Doo Dah Parade (1, B2)
A wacky parody of the Rose Bowl parade with Dead Rose Queens, precision drill briefcase teams, a roving volleyball game and the inimitable antics of the drag-queen WeHo Cheerleaders.
☎ 626-795-9311 💻 www.pasadenadoodahparade.com
✉ Colorado Blvd, Pasadena
⏰ Sun before Thanksgiving
🚇 Memorial Park ♿ good

Museum of Jurassic Technology (3, C3)
Exhibits have nothing to do with dinosaurs and you'll find more technology in a bicycle shop. Instead you'll find displays about Cameroonian stink ants, a tribute to trailer parks and a sculpture of Pope John Paul II squished into the eye of a needle.
☎ 310-836-6131
💻 www.mjt.org ✉ 9341 Venice Blvd, Culver City
⑤ $5/2-3 ⏰ 2-8pm Thu, noon-6pm Fri-Sun 🚌 BBB 12

Self-Realization Fellowship Lake Shrine Temple (3, B2)
Whatever negative vibes you've got will evaporate in this garden of serenity opened by a charismatic yogi, with a windmill-turned-chapel, land-locked houseboat and a shrine interring some of Gandhi's ashes.
☎ 310-454-4114
💻 www.yogananda-srf.org
✉ 17190 Sunset Blvd, Pacific Palisades
⑤ donations welcome
⏰ 9am-4:30pm Tue-Sat, 12:30-4:30pm Sun 🚌 MTA 2
♿ some paths

Skeletons in the Closet (3, D2)
The Los Angeles County Coroner's office is just two floors above the morgue. Pick up toe-tag key chains, body-shaped notepads and beach towels with morbid corpse outlines, all ghoulish fun.
☎ 323-343-0760
💻 http://lacstores.co.la.ca.us/coroner
✉ 1104 N Mission Rd, north of E Cesar Chavez Ave, East LA
⏰ 8am-4:30pm Mon-Fri
🚌 MTA 370, 378 ♿ fair

The Doo Dah Parade – it's a California thing

LA FOR CHILDREN

LA is absolutely kid-friendly, thanks to the casual California lifestyle. Only high-end restaurants and B&Bs might turn children away. The movie biz can bring out everyone's inner child, especially **Universal Studios** (p10) and **Disneyland** (p8). Don't forget the **Aquarium of the Pacific** (p25) or the **Los Angeles Zoo** (p26) either. Look for the 🖎 baby icon listed with individual reviews in the Eating, Entertainment and Sleeping chapters for more options. Surf to www.gocitykids.com /choose, then click 'Los Angeles' for more field trips and current events.

Bob Baker Marionette Theatre (7, B3)

Generations of Angelenos have been enthralled with Bob's adorable singing and dancing marionettes and stuffed animals that interact with the young audiences seated on a carpet. It's pure magic.

☎ 213-250-9995 🖳 www .bobbakermarionettes.com ✉ 1345 W 1st St at Glendale Blvd, Echo Park 💲 $10 ⏲ 10:30am Tue-Fri, 2:30pm Sat & Sun (reservations required) 🚍 MTA 14 ♿ fair

California Science Center (3, C3)

This multimedia bonanza of science hijinks should convince anyone that, gee, science *can* be fun. Kids can test their reaction skills in virtual-reality games and even ride out a simulated earthquake. Don't miss Tess, a giant animated techno-doll billed as '50ft of brains, beauty and biology.' The museum is most crowded on weekday mornings.

☎ 323-724-3623 🖳 www .californiasciencecenter.org ✉ 700 State Dr, Exposition Park 💲 free, IMAX $8/5-6 ⏲ 10am-5pm, Air & Space Gallery 11am-4pm 🚍 Dash F 🅿 $6 ♿ good

Kidspace Children's Museum (1, A2)

Near Pasadena's Rose Bowl, this gigantic facility in Brookside Park is full of hands-on exhibits, outdoor gardens for exploring, and kids' activities from earth yoga to Native American storytelling.

☎ 626-449-9144 🖳 www.kidspacemuseum .org ✉ 480 N Arroyo Blvd, Pasadena 💲 $8 ⏲ 9:30am-5pm ♿ partial

Magicopolis (4, A2)

Aspiring Harry Potters will enjoy the sleight-of-hand and mind-boggling illusions performed by pros in this intimate space, with a great shop for all of your wizard supplies.

☎ 310-451-2241 🖳 www.magicopolis.com ✉ 1418 4th St, Santa Monica 💲 90min shows $20-27 ⏲ schedules vary 🚍 BBB 1, 2, 4, 9, 10 ♿ fair

Natural History Museum of Los Angeles County (3, C3)

Inside a veritable warren of exhibition halls are dueling dinosaur dioramas, animated birds in walk-through forests, an insect zoo, and 300lb of natural gold near the gemstone vault. The California and Native American history exhibits are worth seeking out, too.

☎ 213-763-3466 🖳 www.nhm.org ✉ 900 Exposition Blvd, Exposition Park 💲 $9/2-6.50, free 1st Tue ⏲ 9:30am-5pm Mon-Fri, 10am-5pm Sat & Sun 🚍 DASH F 🅿 $6 ♿ excellent

Pacific Park (4, A2)

On Santa Monica Pier, the arcade games and carnival rides may be quaint, but you get knockout ocean vistas atop the world's first solar-powered Ferris wheel. After-dark crowds can be sketchy.

☎ 310-260-8744 🖳 www.pacpark.com ✉ 380 Santa Monica Pier, Santa Monica 💲 single-ride tickets $1.50-4.50, unlimited rides $20/13 ⏲ 11am-11pm Sun-Thu, 11am-12:30am Fri

The Natural History Museum of Los Angeles County (opposite) – anything but the bare bones

& Sat Jun-Aug, shorter hr Sep-May 🚌 Tide Shuttle, BBB 1, 7, 10 ♿ partial

Page Museum & La Brea Tar Pits (5, E5)
Ongoing excavation of La Brea's oozing asphalt pits has yielded over a million fossilized skeleton parts. Many are mounted inside this natural history museum, where you can watch paleontologists examine the remains of dire wolves, prehistoric camels and saber-toothed tigers.
☎ 323-934-7243
🖳 www.tarpits.org
✉ Hancock Park, 5801 Wilshire Blvd, Mid-City
💲 $7/2-4.50, free 1st Tue
🕑 9:30am-5pm Mon-Fri, 10am-5pm Sat & Sun
🚌 MTA 20, 21 🅿 $6
♿ excellent

Roundhouse Aquarium (3, B4)
Youngsters will get a kick out of close encounters with marine animals and tidal

touch pools at this aquatic science lab. You won't fail to be impressed by the 3500-gallon shark tank. Families head upstairs to the interactive Kids Kelp Korner.
☎ 310-379-8117
🖳 www.roundhousemb.com
✉ end of Manhattan Pier, Manhattan Beach 💲 donation $2 🕑 3pm-sunset Mon-Fri, 10am-sunset Sat & Sun
🚇 Redondo, then bus MTA 126 ♿ partial

Santa Monica Pier Aquarium (4, A2)
Operated by the nonprofit environmental group Heal the Bay, here kids get introduced to jellyfish, small sharks and other critters residing in Santa Monica Bay. They'll also learn about marine conservation and pet sea urchins and sea stars.
☎ 310-393-6149
🖳 www.healthebay.org /smpa ✉ 1600 Ocean Front Walk, below carousel, Santa Monica Pier 💲 donation $5/1

🕑 2-6pm Tue-Fri, 12:30-6pm Sat & Sun Jun-Aug, shorter hr Sep-May
🚌 Tide Shuttle, BBB 1, 7, 10
♿ partial

Six Flags Magic Mountain (2, B2)
Velocity is king at SoCal's 'Xtreme' theme park, where the ever-growing arsenal of thrill rides, shows and attractions includes 16 roller coasters that will scare the bejesus out of you. Traditionalists like Revolution, the first 360-degree giant loop ever built. Entertain younger (and shorter) kids next door at the Hurricane Harbor water park.
☎ 818-367-5965
🖳 www.sixflags.com
✉ 26101 Magic Mountain Pkwy, Valencia 💲 $48/30, Hurricane Harbor $24/17, combo entry $58
🕑 seasonal schedules vary
🚌 I-5 35 miles north of downtown LA 🚌 Starline Tours (p37) 🅿 $10
♿ some rides accessible

Trips & Tours

DRIVING TOUR
Seeing Stars

Maps to stars' homes are sold on Hollywood Blvd, but are often out-of-date. Most stars live behind security gates and high hedges with video surveillance systems, armed patrols and attack dogs – look, but don't trespass.

Which way to the Witch's House?

Drive by **Spadena House** (**1**; 516 Walden Dr), nicknamed the 'Witch's House,' which was spirited off a pre-1930s movie set. Turn right on Carmelita Ave, then right again onto Bedford Dr, a favorite with celebrities since 'It' girl Clara Bow reputedly did scandalous things at **No 512** (**2**). Make a U-turn. Drive up the street to where Steve Martin once resided at **No 721** (**3**) and Stan Laurel lived at **No 718** (**4**). At the corner, **No 730** (**5**) was where Lana Turner's daughter stabbed her mother's abusive lover to death in 1958. Turn left on Lomitas Ave, then right on Linden Dr. Gangster Bugsy Siegel was gunned down at his mistress's house, **No 810** (**6**), in 1947.

Continue north to Sunset Blvd. Drive east to Roxbury Dr, turning left for a lineup of stars' former homes: Lucile Ball at **No 1000** (**7**); Jack Benny at **No 1002** (**8**); Peter 'Columbo' Falk at **No 1004** (**9**); Diane Keaton at **No 1015** (**10**); and Ira and George Gershwin at **Nos 1019 & 1021** (**11**), respectively.

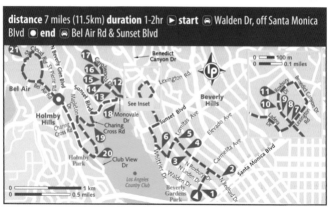

distance 7 miles (11.5km) **duration** 1-2hr ▶ **start** 🚗 Walden Dr, off Santa Monica Blvd ● **end** 🚗 Bel Air Rd & Sunset Blvd

Beverly – Hills, that is. Swimmin' pools, movie stars...

Turn right on Benedict Canyon Dr, right at Lexington Rd, and right again onto Ladera Dr. Veer left onto Monovale Dr; **No 144** (**12**) was Elvis Presley's home. Drive onto Carolwood Dr, another 'celebrity row.' **No 245** (**13**) was occupied by the late Beatle George Harrison. Barbra Streisand once lived at **No 301** (**14**) and Clark Gable at **No 325** (**15**), not far from Walt Disney's estate at **No 355** (**16**). Rod Stewart had to fend off fans from **No 391** (**17**).

Turn around and take Carolwood Dr south back to Sunset Blvd. Off to the left, you can glimpse **Owlwood** (**18**; 141 Carolwood Dr), variously owned by Marilyn Monroe, Tony Curtis, and Sonny and Cher. Drive west on Sunset Blvd, taking the first marked left-turn lane onto Charing Cross Rd down to Hugh Hefner's infamous **Playboy Mansion** (**19**; 10236 Charing Cross Rd). At Mapleton Dr, head left all the way past **No 594** (**20**), TV producer Aaron Spelling's mansion.

Take the next right onto Club View Dr, down to Beverly Glen Blvd. Drive northwest, straight over Sunset Blvd and through the gates of swank Bel Air.

Follow winding Bel Air Rd – where Alfred Hitchcock, Howard Hughes and Judy Garland all lived – up to **No 668** (**21**), where ex-President Ronald Reagan died in 2004. His wife, Nancy, had the original address (No 666) changed because of its satanic associations.

Bugsy Siegel's mistress's house (opposite)

WALKING TOUR
Dabbling in Downtown

Start your daytime walk at gorgeous art-deco **Union Station** (**1**), one of the last grand railway stations built in the USA. Cross the street to **El Pueblo de Los Angeles** (**2**; p18). Walk up narrow **Olvera St** (**3**; p18), stopping in at Xococafé (p62).

Keep going north to **Phillipe the Original** (**4**; p47), then hop on DASH minibus B or DD (p84) up to **Gin Ling Way** (**5**; p18), opposite **Chung King Rd** (**6**; p18).

Ride the bus back down to **City Hall** (**7**; p19). Stroll south, then head east along 1st St for a taste of Little Tokyo at **Fugetsu-do** (**8**; p44) and a cultural infusion at the **Japanese American National Museum** (**9**; p20).

Take DASH minibus A or DD over to **Walt Disney Concert Hall** (**10**; p23), then walk across Grand Ave to the **Museum of Contemporary Art** (**11**; p21).

Cross back over to the **Wells Fargo Center** (**12**; p19). Exiting onto Hope St, turn left to get to the top of the **Bunker Hill Steps** (**13**; p19). Descend to LA's **Central Library** (**14**; p23).

Meander through the Maguire Gardens onto Flower St, then head down to the Standard hotel's **Rooftop Bar** (**15**; p59) for skyscraper views.

distance 2 miles (3km), plus short bus rides **duration** 4hr ▶ **start** ⊚ Union Station ⦿ **end** ⊚ 7th St/Metro Center

The signs are good at the Museum of Contemporary Art (MOCA)

DAY TRIPS
Orange County & San Diego Coasts (2 & 3)

Surfers, artists and carefree dot-com millionaires give Orange County and San Diego's beach towns their enlivening vibe.

Along the Pacific Coast Hwy (Hwy 1), south of old-fashioned downtown Seal Beach, Bolsa Chica State Beach lies opposite wetlands that are a birders' paradise. Huntington Beach is a surf mecca, with its **International Surfing Museum** (☎ 714-960-3483; 411 Olive Ave; $2/1; ☉ noon-5pm Thu-Mon, daily in summer).

Yacht-filled Newport Beach has the Balboa Peninsula's white-sand beaches and hilltop **Orange County Museum of Art** (☎ 949-759-1122; 850 San Clemente Dr; $10/8; ☉ 11am-5pm Tue-Sun, to 8pm Thu). Low-key Laguna Beach revels in its secluded oceanfront, leafy streets, art galleries and festivals (p57).

South of Dana Point, detour inland to historic **Mission San Juan Capistrano** (☎ 949-234-1300; 31882 Camino Capistrano; $6/4-5; ☉ 8:30am-5pm), with lush gardens and graceful arches. South American swallows return here every year around March 19.

Enter San Diego County, then continue past Oceanside. Dally in meditative Encinitas, ritzy Del Mar or beautiful La Jolla. Nearby Pacific Beach, Mission Bay boasts the family attraction **SeaWorld** (☎ 800-257-4268; www.seaworld.com; 500 SeaWorld Dr; $51/41; ☉ 10am-5pm, extended summer hr), where killer whale Shamu lives.

Bohemian Ocean Beach is the gateway to Point Loma, a winter whale-watching perch. Watch the sunset at the Hotel del Coronado, a romantic Victorian whimsy where Marilyn Monroe frolicked in the 1950s movie *Some Like It Hot*.

INFORMATION

- 🚗 Santa Monica to Huntington Beach (50 miles), Santa Monica to San Diego (140 miles)
- 💻 www.ocparks.com, www.sandiego.org
- ☉ beaches open until sunset
- ℹ California Welcome Center (☎ 760-721-1101; 928 North Coast Hwy, Oceanside; ☉ 9am-5pm)
- ✕ Ramos House Café (☎ 949-443-1342; 31752 Los Rios St, San Juan Capistrano); Prince of Wales (☎ 619-435-6611; Hotel del Coronado, 1500 Orange Ave, Coronado)

Messin' around in boats, San Diego Harbor

Santa Barbara & The Wine Country (2)

The refined seaside city of Santa Barbara has more of a Mediterranean atmosphere than SoCal surf style. White-stucco adobe buildings with red-tiled roofs are the town's trademark. Fountains of youth flow from local college campuses, including the University of California at Santa Barbara (UCSB), into downtown. The main artery, State St, is packed with diverting shops, eateries and bars.

INFORMATION

- Amtrak (p83) from Union Station ($18-25, 2½-3½hr)
- Santa Barbara Airbus (☎ 800-423-1618; www.santabarbaraairbus.com) to/from LAX ($42, 2½hr); Greyhound (p83) to/from downtown LA ($12, 2¼-3hr)
- Santa Monica to Santa Barbara (90 miles)
- www.santabarbaraca.com, www.sbcountywines.com
- beaches open until sunset
- Santa Barbara Visitors Center (☎ 805-965-3021; 1 Garden St, Santa Barbara; ☺ 9am-6pm Mon-Sat, 10am-5pm Sun)
- Wine Cask (☎ 805-966-9463; 813 Anacapa St, Santa Barbara), Hitching Post II (☎ 805-688-0676; 406 E Hwy 246, Buellton)

The **Santa Barbara Museum of Art** (☎ 805-963-4364; 1130 State St; $9/6-7; ☺ 11am-5pm Tue-Sun) stands nearby the Spanish-Moorish **county courthouse** (☎ 805-962-6464; 1100 Anacapa St; admission free; ☺ 8:30am-4:30pm Mon-Fri, 10am-4:30pm Sat & Sun, tours 2pm Mon-Sat), where you can ascend a clock tower for vistas. Graceful **Mission Santa Barbara** (☎ 805-682-4713; 2201 Laguna St; $4/free; ☺ 9am-5pm) perches north of downtown. Flung further south along the waterfront are more minor maritime attractions.

Santa Barbara's wine country was made famous by the 2004 indie movie *Sideways*. Drive right up into the mountains on curvy Hwy 154 or take US 101 along the coast. Charming Los Olivos has tasting rooms. Wineries are scattered south toward Santa Ynez, where Hwy 246 connects west to Buellton, just off US 101, via the bizarrely incongruous Danish outpost of Solvang.

On a mission out of LA – Mission Santa Barbara

ORGANIZED TOURS

Thanks to SoCal's mellow climate, most tours operate year-round. On Hollywood Blvd, touts hawk seats for tours of stars' homes (p32). Other van and bus tours take in city overviews or amusement parks. For TV and movie studio tours, see p27. For whale-watching cruises, see p26.

Architecture Tours LA

If architecture is your thing, you can tool around town in the comfort of an air-con minivan while taking in styles from Arts & Crafts to Mid-Century Modern. Your knowledgeable guide is an expert in the evolution of post-modern architecture in LA.
☎ 323-464-7868 🖳 www.architecturetoursla.com 💲 tours per person from $65 🕑 schedules vary (reservations required)

Gondola Getaway (3, D5)

Romantic rides in authentic Italian gondolas on the canals of Naples (California, that is). Gondoliers provide a picnic basket, you bring the wine. Make reservations early, especially for sunset and full-moon cruises.
☎ 562-433-9595 🖳 www.gondolagetawayinc.com ✉ 5437 E Ocean Blvd, Long Beach 💲 50min cruise per couple $65, each additional person $15, plus tip 🕑 11am-11pm (reservations required)

LA Conservancy

Join docents every Saturday morning downtown for nonprofit art and architectural tours of art-deco buildings, old Broadway movie palaces and more. Proceeds help save these historic structures from the wrecking ball.
☎ 213-623-2489 🖳 www.laconservancy.org ✉ locations vary 💲 2hr tours $10 🕑 call for hr (reservations required)

Neon Cruises (7, A5)

The brainchild of the Museum of Neon Art (p19), these nighttime neon tours in open-air, double-decker buses always sell out, so book well ahead.
☎ 213-489-9918 🖳 www.neonmona.org ✉ 501 W Olympic Blvd, downtown LA 💲 3hr tours $45 🕑 usually 7:30pm Sat Jun-Oct (reservations required)

Red Line Tours (5, B1)

Walking tours of Hollywood and downtown LA use live headsets that cut out traffic noise. The guides use a clever mix of anecdotes, fun facts, trivia and historical and architectural informa-tion to keep everyone entertained.
☎ 323-402-1074 🖳 www.redlinetours.com ✉ 6773 Hollywood Blvd, Hollywood 💲 1¼hr tours $20/15-18 🕑 tours daily (reservations required)

Starline Tours (5, A1)

One of the behemoth opera-tors, Starline offers pick-ups from major hotels for bus trips to amusement parks. Tours of stars' homes depart frequently from Grauman's Chinese Theatre (p65).
☎ 800-959-3131 🖳 www.starlinetours.com ✉ 6801 Hollywood Blvd, Hollywood 💲 1hr tours $16/12, full-day tours from $79/61 🕑 several tours daily

Urban Shopping Adventures

Personal concierges will es-cort you around downtown's Fashion District (p40) or chic Melrose Ave boutiques. You'll enjoy special discounts, too.
☎ 213-683-9715 🖳 www.urbanshoppingadventures.com 💲 tours $35-190 🕑 call for hr (reservations required)

'Ciao, dude.' A slice of Italy in California.

Shopping

Shopping is a joy for every LA fashionista. Although boutique staff often shower attention only on rich and famous faces, don't let yourself be cowed. Remember, SoCal is the birthplace of the middle-brow shopping mall.

Major sales clear out end-of-season merchandise, like summer wear being heavily discounted in early August. The biggest shopping frenzies start early the mornings after Thanksgiving and Christmas. Designers' sample sales are held year-round, so ask around.

When perusing price tags, remember to add 8.25% sales tax. It's the rare store that doesn't accept plastic cards or readily offer refunds for merchandise with the tags still attached if you change your mind. Many stores offer valet parking or validations for lots and garages.

Typical shopping hours are 11am to 6pm daily, except Sunday (usually noon to 5pm). Malls and megastores stay open later, till 9pm or so most days. Some supermarkets, pharmacies and convenience stores are open 24 hours.

Shopping Areas

Beverly Hills beckons with international couture and jewelry, especially along Rodeo Dr (5, A5). Cutting-edge designer boutiques line Robertson Blvd (5, C4) south of Beverly Blvd, with sassy fashions on Melrose Ave (5, E4), west of La Brea Ave.

East of Hollywood, Los Feliz's Vermont Ave (5, G6) and Silver Lake's Sunset Junction (5, H6) mix up vintage clothing stores, vinyl record shops and more eccentric finds. In West Hollywood, look to upscale Sunset Plaza (5, C3).

Downtown LA's Olvera St (7, C4) sells Mexican crafts, while Chinatown's kitschy Central Plaza (7, C3) deals in Asian imports. Designer knockoffs and crazy bargains abound in the Fashion District (7, B5).

Of the beach towns, Santa Monica is best: the chain-laden Third Street Promenade (4, A2), tony Montana Ave (4, B1) and one-of-a-kind Main St (4, A3). Venice's eclectic Abbot Kinney Blvd (4, A4) vends antiques, art and fashion. For cheap and crazy souvenirs, haggle on Ocean Front Walk (4, A4).

Sun, surf...and shopping in LA

DEPARTMENT STORES & MALLS

Barneys New York (5, A5)
Svelte and stylish, Barneys carries newly minted fashions and classic designers. Stop by Chelsea Passage for artisan gifts or the acclaimed rooftop deli, Barney Greengrass, for views of the Hollywood Hills.
☎ 310-276-4400 ✉ 9570 Wilshire Blvd, Beverly Hills
☼ 10am-7pm Mon-Sat, to 8pm Thu, noon-6pm Sun
🚌 MTA 720
🅿 2hr validated free

Beverly Center (5, C4)
Despite the Soviet-style exterior, this is LA's glamour mall, the place you're most likely to spot a celebrity, anyone from Beyoncé to Mark Wahlberg. Show your hotel key at guest services for discounts, then lose yourself in over 130 boutique shops and department stores.
☎ 310-854-0071 ✉ 8500 Beverly Blvd, Mid-City
☼ 10am-9pm Mon-Fri, 10am-8pm Sat, 11am-6pm Sun
🚌 DASH Fairfax 🅿 3hr $1

Century City
A divine alfresco shopping mall, and it's only a mile from Rodeo Dr. Godiva chocolates, Kenneth Cole and Abercrombie & Fitch are among over 100 mostly high-end stores anchored by Bloomingdale's and Macy's.
☎ 310-277-3898 ✉ 10250 Santa Monica Blvd, Century City ☼ 10am-9pm Mon-Sat, 11am-6pm Sun 🚌 MTA 316, BBB 5 🅿 3hr free

Citadel Outlets (3, D3)
Even if stores like Calvin Klein and Tommy Hilfiger didn't offer discounts up to 70% off retail prices, it would still be worth the drive. A few dozen shops stand behind the Assyrian palace backdrop from the epic movie *Ben Hur*.
☎ 323-888-1724 ✉ 5675 E Telegraph Rd, Commerce
☼ 10am-8pm Mon-Sat, 10am-6pm Sun 🚌 MTA 362
🚄 I-5 7 miles south of downtown LA, exit Atlantic Blvd N 🅿 free

Hollywood & Highland (5, A1)
A perfect marriage of kitsch and commerce, this high-powered shopping and entertainment complex is the spark plug for Hollywood Blvd's rebirth. Standing next to Grauman's Chinese Theatre (p65), the shops and eateries here are mostly of the chain variety, except for Wolfgang Puck's Vert (p48).
☎ 323-467-6412 ✉ 6801 Hollywood Blvd, Hollywood
☼ 10am-10pm Mon-Sat, 10am-7pm Sun ⊕ Hollywood/Highland 🚌 DASH Hollywood
🅿 4hr validated $2

Santa Monica Place (4, A2)
In a Frank Gehry–designed structure at the end of Third St Promenade, this galleria has pedestrian chain shops and a few designers. Out-of-town visitors can get discount cards from guest services near the fast-food court.
☎ 310-394-1049 ✉ 395 Santa Monica Pl, Santa Monica
☼ 10am-9pm Mon-Sat, 11am-6pm Sun 🚌 Tide Shuttle, BBB 1-5, 7-10
🅿 3hr free, after 5pm Thu-Sat $3

Hollywood and Highland – look up for a sign from above

CLOTHING, SHOES & JEWELRY

American Apparel (5, A1)
Ragingly stylish but blessedly logo-free T-shirts, tank tops, skirts and shorts in a rainbow of colors – everything is cut and sewn from high-quality cotton right in downtown LA in a sweatshop-free facility. There are several branches around town.
☎ 323-465-6312 🖳 www .americanapparel.net
✉ 6922 Hollywood Blvd, Hollywood ⏱ 11am-9pm Mon-Thu, 11am-10pm Fri & Sat, 11am-7pm Sun
🚇 Hollywood/Highland

Decades (5, D4)
A passion for 1960s and '70s couture and accessories keeps this gorgeous style emporium stocked with Pucci, Chanel and other design legends. The top quality attracts Industry stylists and even celebrities. Downstairs at Decades Two, you can stock up on barely worn contemporary looks.
☎ 323-655-1960 ✉ 8214 Melrose Ave, Mid-City
⏱ 11:30am-6pm Mon-Sat, noon-5pm Sun
🚌 DASH Fairfax

Fred Segal (5, D4)
Cameron Diaz and Nicole Kidman are among the stars dressed by this kingpin of LA fashion boutiques that doubles as a launchpad for new designers. Here a jewel box of mini stores vend clothing, shoes and more, along with an on-site salon, spa and café. Cash-strapped fashionistas invade during the half-off sale, usually in late September. Also on Broadway in Santa Monica (4, A2).
☎ 323-651-1800 ✉ 8100 Melrose Ave, West Hollywood
⏱ 10am-7pm Mon-Sat, noon-6pm Sun 🚌 DASH Fairfax 🅿 free lot

Harry Winston (5, A5)
If you're ready to seriously swoon, hit the buzzer to enter the glittering storefront of the ultimate diamond purveyor to the stars, who loans out millions of dollars' worth of gems every Oscar night. Ben Affleck picked out J.Lo's infamous pink-diamond engagement ring here.
☎ 310-271-8554 ✉ 371 N Rodeo Dr, Beverly Hills
⏱ 10am-6pm Mon-Fri, 11am-5pm Sat 🚌 MTA 720

It's a Wrap! (5, C6)
This superb secondhand shop resells TV- and movie-studio production clothes. Up-to-the-minute designer fashions are in mint condition, having been worn only once or

You can buy warmer clothes at American Apparel, too!

twice (or not at all!). All sizes, all styles for both men and women, hang on the racks. Also in Burbank (3, C2; ☎ 818-567-7366; 3315 W Magnolia Blvd).
☎ 310-246-9727
🖳 www.movieclothes.com
✉ 1164 S Robertson Blvd
⏱ 11am-8pm Mon-Fri, 11am-6pm Sat & Sun
🚌 MTA 220, BBB 5, 7, 12

Kitson (5, C4)
Stay ahead of the fashion curve by popping into this hip haven chock-full of tomorrow's outfits, many of them with locally made labels. Kitson also stocks

FLOCKING FOR FASHION
Clothes horses will love the Fashion District (7, B5), a frantic 90-block warren of downtown LA. It's fun, but first-timers can find the district bewildering. To orient yourself, browse the website (www.fashiondistrict.org) and print out a map of the area. Skip stores marked Mayoreo, or 'Wholesale Only,' and bring cash. Do not expect exchanges, refunds or to get more than 10% to 20% off with polite haggling. Most shops are open 10am to 5pm Monday to Saturday. Designer knockoffs are sold daily in Santee Alley and New Alley (enter off 11th St, between Maple Ave and Santee St).

CLOTHING & SHOE SIZES

Women's Clothing

Aust/UK	8	10	12	14	16	18
Europe	36	38	40	42	44	46
Japan	5	7	9	11	13	15
USA	6	8	10	12	14	16

Women's Shoes

Aust/USA	5	6	7	8	9	10
Europe	35	36	37	38	39	40
France only	35	36	38	39	40	42
Japan	22	23	24	25	26	27
UK	3½	4½	5½	6½	7½	8½

Men's Clothing

Aust	92	96	100	104	108	112
Europe	46	48	50	52	54	56

Japan	S	M	M		L	
UK/USA	35	36	37	38	39	40

Men's Shirts (Collar Sizes)

Aust/Japan	38	39	40	41	42	43
Europe	38	39	40	41	42	43
UK/USA	15	15½	16	16½	17	17½

Men's Shoes

Aust/UK	7	8	9	10	11	12
Europe	41	42	43	44½	46	47
Japan	26	27	27.5	28	29	30
USA	7½	8½	9½	10½	11½	12½

Measurements approximate only; try before you buy.

goodies designed by famous faces, such as Tokyo-inspired tees by Gwen Stefani and girlish bags by Nicky Hilton, plus fun nostalgia wear like Tinkerbell tank tops and Curious George cashmere.
☎ 310-859-2652 ✉ 115 S Robertson Blvd, West Hollywood 🕙 10am-7pm Mon-Sat, 11am-6pm Sun 🚌 DASH Fairfax

Lisa Kline (5, C4)
Nubile size 0-6s will fall in love with slipknotted tanks, sparkling knits and suede pants from pop designers such as Juicy Couture and Paper Denim. Watch out for a 'no touch' policy on some items. Star boys head across the street to Lisa Kline Men at No 123, while youthful shoppers rave about the outlet on Melrose Ave (5, F4).
☎ 310-246-0907 ✉ 136 S Robertson Blvd, West Hollywood 🕙 11am-7pm Mon-Sat, noon-6pm Sun 🚌 DASH Fairfax

Moondance (4, B1)
This skylit gallery is the go-to place for handmade artisan

jewelry by A-list contemporary designers. No refunds are given.
☎ 310-395-5516 ✉ 1530 Montana Ave, Santa Monica 🕙 10am-6pm Mon-Sat, 11am-5pm Sun 🚌 BBB 3

Re-Mix Vintage Shoes (5, E4)
It collects never-worn vintage and reproduction footwear from the 1940s to '60s, if you should need baby-doll pumps or two-tone wing tips to complete your fab retro look.
☎ 323-936-6210 ✉ 7605 Beverly Blvd, Mid-City

🕙 noon-7pm Mon-Sat, noon-6pm Sun 🚌 MTA 14

Wasteland (5, E4)
This vintage warehouse has glamour gowns, velvet suits and all manner of other retro outfits dating back to the '40s, as well as rows of racks packed with last season's designer styles, all at reasonable prices. It's a favorite haunt of club kids.
☎ 323-653-3028 ✉ 7428 Melrose Ave, Mid-City 🕙 11am-8pm Mon-Sat, 11am-7pm Sun 🚌 MTA 10, 11

Why, thank you! Can I sign an autograph for you?

MUSIC & BOOKS

Amoeba Music (5, G2)
Hailing from the San Francisco Bay area, independent Amoeba has made a big splash in Hollywood. All-star staff and listening stations help you sort through over half a million new and used CDs, DVDs, videos and vinyl. Free in-store live shows.
☎ 323-245-6400 ✉ 6400 W Sunset Blvd, Hollywood ⏰ 10:30am-11pm Mon-Sat, 11am-9pm Sun 🚌 MTA 2

Aron's Records (5, F3)
Since 1965 Aron's has been pleasing customers with racks of new and used CDs and vinyl from the lands of punk, rock, electronica, world beat, jazz and blues, and beyond. Biannual parking-lot sales are legendary.
☎ 323-469-4700 ✉ 1150 N Highland Ave, Hollywood ⏰ 10am-10pm Sun-Thu, 10am-midnight Fri & Sat 🚌 MTA 156 🅿 free lot

Bodhi Tree (5, C4)
Spiritual folks gravitate to this tranquil dispensary of meditation pillows, soulful tomes, music and incense. Psychics often offer readings (from $20) on the walkway next to the store.
☎ 310-659-1733 ✉ 8585 Melrose Ave, West Hollywood

⏰ 10am-11pm, annex 10am-7pm 🚌 DASH Hollywood/West Hollywood 🅿 valet $3.50

Book Soup (5, C3)
Screenwriters, rock 'n' roll stars and prize-winning authors sign autographs here on the Sunset Strip. Film and fashion books, queer studies and pulp fiction almost fly off the shelves. The annex stacks used books, while the outdoor newsstand sells international papers and cult 'zines.
☎ 310-659-3110 ✉ 8818 Sunset Blvd, West Hollywood ⏰ 9am-10pm Mon-Sat, 9am-7pm Sun, annex & newsstand shorter hr 🚌 MTA 2 🅿 free lot behind store

Koma Books (7, A4)
La bibliotèque infernale specializes in the most warped, bizarre, sleazy, controversial and anarchic material ever committed to print. This includes murderers' diaries, Japanese porn, drug literature…nothing is off-limits.
☎ 213-623-6995 ✉ 1228 W 7th St, downtown LA ⏰ call for hr 🚌 DASH E

Larry Edmunds Bookshop (5, B1)
Dig here for movie scripts, posters, lobby cards and

What's stirring at Book Soup?

trashy biographies of the stars. A serious tome on the making of *Blade Runner* may rub spines with voyeuristic blood-and-guts histories of Hollywood here.
☎ 323-463-3273 ✉ 6644 Hollywood Blvd, Hollywood ⏰ 10am-5:30pm 🚇 Hollywood/Highland

Vinyl Fetish (5, C2)
This store is nirvana for the turntable brigade with classic and hot releases in house, trance, jungle, punk, industrial and more esoteric sounds. In-the-know staff happily sell DJ gear, and a handful of players stand by for trial listening.
☎ 323-957-2290 ✉ 1614 N Cahuenga Blvd, Hollywood ⏰ noon-8pm 🚌 DASH Hollywood

READING LA
For the morbidly inclined, *Death in Paradise: An Illustrated History of the Los Angeles County Department of Coroner*, by Tony Blanche & Brad Schreiber, looks at the crime-solving heroics behind sensational cases of celebrity demise. Laurie Jacobson's *Dishing Hollywood: The Real Scoop on Tinseltown's Most Notorious Scandals* is another guilty pleasure. *The Other Hollywood: The Uncensored Oral History of the Porn Film Industry*, by Legs McNeil et al, talks to an encyclopedia's worth of XXX stars and traces the rise of porno chic. For more literary books and cultural critics, see p81.

FOR CHILDREN

La La Ling (5, G5)
Hip parents will tote their tots to this self-proclaimed 'contemporary baby lifestyle boutique' selling concert T-shirts by Claude, layered Indian skirts by Devi and lil' Harley Davidson dresses.
☎ 323-664-4400 ✉ 1810 N Vermont Ave, Los Feliz ⏱ 10am-7pm Mon-Sat, 11am-4pm Sun 🚌 DASH Hollywood

Meltdown Comics & Collectibles (5, E2)
Bright lights beckon off Sunset Blvd. Inside, mainstream comics sit beside indie graphic novels and limited-edition art. In the kids' section are Hello Kitty goods and exclusive tees.
☎ 323-851-7223 ✉ 7522 W Sunset Blvd, West Hollywood ⏱ 11am-10pm Thu-Tue, 10am-10pm Wed 🚌 DASH Hollywood/West Hollywood

Munky King (7, C3)
Specializing in independent designer toys from around the world, this toy temple with a twist has an inventory more suitable to teens and adults than tots: here you will find urban vinyl toys, bizarre stuffed animals and other alternative playthings.
☎ 213-620-8787 ✉ 441 Gin Ling Way, downtown LA ⏱ noon-7pm Mon-Thu, noon-8pm Fri, 11am-9pm Sat, 11am-7pm Sun 🚌 DASH B

Puzzle Zoo (4, A2)
Low-tech wooden trains will tempt the little ones, while the older kids are mesmerized by hard-to-find action figures and mind-bending 3-D puzzles. There's also a store at the Beverly Center (p39) in Mid-City.
☎ 310-393-9201 ✉ 1413 Third St Promenade, Santa Monica ⏱ 10am-10pm Sun-Thu, 10am-midnight Fri & Sat 🚌 BBB 1, 7, 8

Don't have a meltdown – take 'em to Meltdown

Wound & Wound Toy Co (6, B2)
No one can resist fiddling with the wild universe of wind-up toys found here. Each toy costs just a few dollars, even the tiny human brain that hops along the counter. They also sell hurdy-gurdy music boxes and tin toys.
☎ 818-509-8129 ✉ 100 Universal Plaza, Universal City Walk ⏱ 11am-9pm Sun-Thu, 11am-11pm Fri & Sat Ⓜ Universal City

There's lots of toy stories at Wound & Wound Toy Co

FOOD & DRINK

Many specialty food shops can be found in ethnic neighborhoods, especially in downtown LA (p18).

Cheese Store of Beverly Hills (5, A5)

Take your pick from fragrant goat cheeses, creamy bries, crumbly blues, smoky goudas and other familiar and exotic cheeses, most of them handcrafted, that are temptingly displayed at this quaint little cheese store. Staff will happily advise customers.

☎ 310-278-2855 ✉ 419 N Beverly Dr, Beverly Hills
🕑 10am-6pm Mon-Sat
🚌 MTA 720

Compartes (3, B3)

Even Frank Sinatra loved these signature redwood boxes of sweet glacé California fruit hand-dipped in chocolate, costing from $20 per pound (free samples are available). Bags of exotic truffles dissolve diet willpower.

☎ 310-826-3380 ✉ 912 S Barrington Ave, at San Vicente Blvd, Brentwood
🕑 10am-5:30pm Mon-Fri, 11am-5:30pm Sat 🚌 BBB 4

Fugetsu-do (7, C4)

For over a hundred years, skilled family bakers at this Little Tokyo sweet shop have been making confections like *manju* (sweet bean cakes) and *mochi* (pounded rice taffy).

☎ 213-625-8595 ✉ 315 E 1st St, downtown LA
🕑 8am-6pm Sun-Thu, 8am-7pm Fri & Sat 🚌 DASH A, DD

SPECIALIST STORES

Hustler Hollywood (5, C3)

'Relax – it's just sex' is the motto of this emporium of erotica conceived by the daughter of porno purveyor Larry Flynt. XXX-rated videos star the people who might just be standing next to you at the coffee bar.

☎ 310-860-9009 ✉ 8920 Sunset Blvd, West Hollywood
🕑 10am-2am 🚌 MTA 2

Off the Wall Antiques (5, F4)

Every wacky collectible here is fabulously priced. Gawk at 1950s robot toys, vintage carnival paraphernalia or neon signs, all in tip-top condition.

☎ 323-930-1185 ✉ 7325 Melrose Ave, Mid-City

🕑 11am-6pm Mon-Sat
🚌 MTA 10, 11

Rock'er Board Shop

For babes who skate and surf (but your man is welcome, too), this indie shop has cutting-edge, often locally designed gear and puts on special events like 'Tattoo Your Board' night with Venice artists. They even give surf lessons (per hour $60-75). Rock on, sisters.

☎ 310-397-8300 ✉ 12204 Venice Blvd, west of I-405, Mar Vista
🕑 11am-7pm Mon-Fri, 10am-6pm Sat, 11-5pm Sun
🚌 MTA 33, 333

Splash Bath & Body (4, A3)

All-natural, luscious bath products are definitely worth every penny. Throw a cocoa-butter bath bomb into your hotel tub, or apply a lemonade rinse for clearer skin. The staff are generous with free product samples. There's also a store at Hermosa Beach (3, C4).

☎ 310-581-4200 ✉ 2823 Main St, Santa Monica
🕑 11am-7pm Mon-Thu, 10am-8pm Fri & Sat, 10am-7pm Sun
🚌 Tide Shuttle, BBB 1

DON'T FLEE!

LA is bursting with trendy flea markets. Show up early, and bring cash (small bills are best) and lots of shopping karma to:

Melrose Trading Post (5, E4; Fairfax High School, 7850 Melrose Ave, West Hollywood; entry $2; 9am-5pm Sun) A hipster market with everything from bangles to badminton rackets.

Peddler on the Roof (5, H2; 1423 Gordon St, Hollywood; entry $3; noon-5pm Sat) DJs spin while you snap up groovy goods.

Rose Bowl Flea Market (1, A1; Rose Bowl, Brookside Park, Pasadena; public entry after 9am $7; 7:30am-3pm every 2nd Sun of the month) Thousands of antique and secondhand vendors.

Eating

Eating in LA's culinary temples is not just a way to fill your stomach, it's also a way to see and be seen. New restaurants baptized by stars (or equally famous chefs) are certain to survive and thrive – at least, momentarily.

Evolved in part by LA's own Wolfgang Puck back in the 1980s, California cuisine focuses on fresh, seasonal ingredients and unusual flavor fusions, with such offshoots as Cal-Asian and Nuevo Latino specialties. Vegetarians and those with other dietary restrictions are easily accommodated. For gourmet food shops, see opposite.

Surprisingly, downtown LA has one of the city's most vibrant dining scenes. Glamorous crowds feast in West Hollywood and Beverly Hills, while Venice and Santa Monica have proven their culinary creativity. Recently, red-hot eateries (often with celebrity co-owners) have arisen in Hollywood, and certain Mid-City streets have become foodie meccas.

MEAL COSTS

The pricing symbols used in this chapter indicate the average cost of a main course at dinner, without drinks, taxes or tip.

$	under $10
$$	$10-18
$$$	$19-30
$$$$	over $30

For a prime table, make reservations in advance to avoid waiting or being turned away. Dining early or ordering at the bar also works. Valet parking is available at many restaurants. Children are typically allowed, except at high-end places. Smoking is illegal indoors. Wheelchair access is easily available at the restaurants listed in this chapter only where the ♿ icon is displayed.

Most restaurants open for lunch (11am to 2:30pm) and dinner (5:30pm to 9:30pm, later on weekends). If restaurants take a day off, it's Monday. A few specialize in breakfast or serve weekend brunch. Diners and coffee shops sometimes stay open 24 hours.

Many restaurants are fully licensed to serve alcohol, unless they say 'BYOB.' Corkage fees vary up to around $15 per bottle. As California is a premier wine-producing region, house wines hold to a high standard.

See p91 for tipping.

'On a clear day you can see the bottom of this wine glass!' Moonshadows restaurant (p54).

DOWNTOWN LA

Downtown probably feeds more people than anywhere else in LA, and the food is surprisingly good. For regional specialties from Szechuan to Hokkaido, just follow your nose along Chinatown's Broadway or 1st St in Little Tokyo.

Café Pinot (7, B4)
Californian $$$
Outside LA's beautiful Central Library, this indoor/outdoor eatery run by Patina chef Joachim Splichal serves sophisticated, fresh contemporary fare amidst the Maguire Gardens. Make reservations.
☎ 213-239-6500 ✉ 700 W 5th St ⏱ 11:30am-2:30pm Mon-Fri, 5-9pm Mon-Tue, 5-9:30pm Wed-Thu, 5-10pm

Go for gold at the Cicada

Fri-Sat, 4:30-9pm Sun
🚌 DASH A, B, C, DD, F ♿

Cicada (7, B5)
Northern Italian $$$
A theatrical space inside the art-deco Oviatt Building, this ravishing restaurant has gold-leaf ceilings and curved black leather booths. Dress up to dine on shrimp or smoked-duck ravioli, followed by masterful secondi and after-dinner grappa. Service is refined. Reservations advised.
☎ 213-488-9488 ✉ 617 S Olive St ⏱ 5:30-9pm Mon-Sat
🚌 DASH B, C ♿

Ciudad (7, B4)
Nuevo Latino $$$
The TV-chef team of Mary Sue Milliken and Susan Feniger pioneer a pan–Latin American menu with all the colors and tastes of *carnaval*. Stop by during the very happy hour

for *mojitos* (rum cocktails) and *cuchifrito* (snacks). Make reservations for dinner.
☎ 213-486-5171 ✉ 445 S Figueroa St ⏱ 11:30am-3pm Mon-Fri, happy hour 3-7pm Mon-Fri & 4-9pm Sun, dinner from 5pm nightly
🚇 7th St/Metro Center
🚌 DASH A, DD, F ♿

Empress Pavilion (7, C3)
Chinese/Dim Sum $$
This Hong Kong–style banquet hall has seating for a small village (500 people, to be exact). Delicacies just fly off the carts wheeled to your table by a small army of servers. Off the regular menu, seafood rarely disappoints. The bakery and take-out counter serve sweets and tea.
☎ 213-617-9898
✉ Bamboo Plaza, 988 N Hill St ⏱ 9am-10pm Mon-Fri, 8am-2pm & 5-10pm Sat & Sun
🚌 DASH B, DD
Ⓟ validated garage ♿

Grand Central Market (7, B4)
International $
In a 1905 beaux arts building, where architect Frank Lloyd Wright once kept an office, this frenzied bazaar is an international nibbler's delight. Head straight to Maria's Pescado Frito for great fish tacos or El Gaucho for lobster empanadas.
☎ 213-624-2378 ✉ 317 S Broadway ⏱ 9am-6pm
🚇 Pershing Square
🚌 DASH DD Ⓟ 1hr validated free ♿ Ⓥ

La Luz del Día (7, C4)
Mexican $
There's always a line snaking out onto the plaza at this self-service venue in the historic

El Pueblo (p18). The *picadillo* (beef stew) is habit-forming, but you might find the spunky nopales (cactus) salad to your liking, too. Cash only.
☎ 213-628-7495 ✉ 1 Olvera St ⏰ 11am-8pm Tue-Sun 🚌 DASH B, DD 👶

Noé (7, B4)
Eclectic $$$
Master chef Robert Gadsby cooks up a storm at this cool, cobalt outpost inside the Omni Hotel. His restless palate results in New American cuisine, which translates into mimosa salad with crispy chicken and minted mango frappé or an almond 'cloud' with a toasted hazelnut veil. Reservations advised.
☎ 213-356-4100 ✉ 251 S Olive St ⏰ 5-10pm Sun-Thu, 5pm-midnight Fri & Sat 🚌 DASH B, DD 👶

Patina (7, B4)
Cal-French $$$$
In stunning new digs at the Walt Disney Concert Hall (p23), Patina is culinary wunderkind Joachim Splichal's flagship. Tantalize your tongue with unique compositions like grilled scallops in lemon-miso glaze or rib-eye beef with fiddlehead-fern sauté. Make reservations.
☎ 213-972-3331 ✉ 141 S Grand Ave

Polished table manners at Patina

⏰ lunch 11:30am-1:30pm Mon-Fri, dinner 5-9:30pm nightly (to 11pm performance nights) 🚌 DASH A, DD 👶

Philippe the Original (7, C3)
American Classic $
The 'home of the French dip sandwich' (eaten doused in hot, spicy mustard), this sawdust-covered eatery has been dishing up tasty working-class fare since 1908. High-powered lawyers, Chinese aunties and tourists all share the communal bench tables. Coffee costs just 9¢.
☎ 213-628-3781 ✉ 1001 N Alameda St ⏰ 6am-10pm 🚇 Union Station 🚌 DASH B, DD 🅿 free lot 👶 Ⓥ

R-23 (7, D5)
Japanese $
Not even the bold art and Frank Gehry–designed chairs can distract from the exquisite and ultra-fresh piscine treats prepared by a team of sushi masters who aren't chintzy with the smiles – or the cuts. It's a pilgrimage worth making.
☎ 213-687-7178 ✉ 923 E 2nd St ⏰ 11:30am-2pm Mon-Fri, 5:30-10pm Mon-Sat 🚌 DASH A, DD 🅿 metered

Water Grill (7, B4)
Seafood $$$$
Only the brisk ocean breeze is missing from this contemporary seafood restaurant. Eat your way across the Americas, from Maine lobster to Mexican shrimp, or around the world with caviar. Servers and the sommelier take equal pains with every diner. Dress well, and make reservations.
☎ 213-891-0900 ✉ 544 S Grand Ave ⏰ 11:30am-8:30pm Mon & Tue, 11:30am-9:30pm Wed-Fri, 5-9:30pm Sat, 5-8:30pm Sun 🚌 DASH B, C, DD

BEST FOR BIZ
The business of LA *is* entertainment, so finding a place to dine while you do business is easy. Industry-favorite restaurants also trafficked by executives and politicos include Water Grill (right), Spago (p51), Ago (p49) and Hal's Bar & Grill (p53). For power breakfasts, try hotel restaurants like Dakota (p48) and the Polo Lounge at the Beverly Hills Hotel (p13), or Kate Mantilini (p51).

HOLLYWOOD, LOS FELIZ & SILVER LAKE

Dakota (5, A1)
Steakhouse $$$$
At this swank joint just off the low-lit lobby of the Hollywood Roosevelt Hotel (p72), reservations are essential if you want one of the luscious leather and suede banquettes. The mod menu ranges from classic chops to truffle mac 'n' cheese.
☎ 323-769-8888 ✉ Roosevelt Hotel, 7000 Hollywood Blvd, Hollywood ⏲ 6-11am & 11:30am-2:30pm daily, 6-11pm Sun-Thu, 6pm-midnight Fri & Sat 🚇 Hollywood/Highland 🅿 validated $6 🚻

El Conquistador (5, H6)
Mexican Cantina $$
In a garden setting straight out of a Mexican fishing village, this sunny respite serves traditional regional dishes, including Sonorose chicken and mole. Festively colored tiles and potent margaritas are bonuses.
☎ 323-666-5136 ✉ 3701 W Sunset Blvd, Silver Lake

⏲ 4-10pm Mon, 11am-10pm Tue-Thu & Sun, 11am-11pm Fri & Sat 🚌 MTA 2, 4 🚻

Fred 62 (5, G5)
American Diner $
This retro-cool diner serves up polyethnic sandwiches, salads and noodles. Even vegans will rejoice. Ooey-gooey breakfast fare, like the Hunka Hunka Burnin' Love Pancake, is dished up all day long.
☎ 323-667-0062 ✉ 1850 N Vermont Ave, Los Feliz ⏲ 24hr 🚌 DASH Los Feliz 🚻 🚻 Ⓥ

Musso & Frank Grill (5, B1)
Steakhouse $$$
Hollywood history hangs thickly in the air at the Boulevard's oldest eatery and once again among its hippest. Red-jacketed waiters balance platters of steaks, chops, grilled liver and other standards. Service is smooth, and so are the martinis. Sit at the counter for company.
☎ 323-467-7788 ✉ 6667 Hollywood Blvd, Hollywood ⏲ 11am-11pm Tue-Sat 🚇 Hollywood/Highland 🚻

Providence (5, G4)
Seafood $$$$
In the lucky spot where Patina (p47) once reigned, the culinary dream team that includes ex–Water Grill (p47) chef Michael Cimarosti seemingly can't fail. Artful nautical decor enhances an encyclopedic menu of fresh bounty from under the sea. Reservations are essential.
☎ 323-460-4170 ✉ 5955 Melrose Ave, Hollywood ⏲ 6-10pm Mon-Sat 🚌 MTA 10, 11 🚻

Skooby's (5, B1)
American Fast Food $
Skooby's gourmet wieners are great, but it's the fries – fresh, crispy and served with a mayo dipping sauce – that give this place an edge. The fresh lemonade is essential, as well.
☎ 323-468-3647 ✉ 6654 Hollywood Blvd, Hollywood ⏲ 11am-midnight Sun-Thu, 11am-3am Fri & Sat 🚇 Hollywood/Highland 🚻 🚻

Vert (5, B1)
Fusion $$-$$$
Wolfgang Puck's paean to Parisian brasseries makes flavor excursions to Italy and California. Settle into a sleek turquoise booth, order the signature Bellini cocktail (prosecco and green apple juice), then look forward to the likes of steak au poivre. Take-out picnic meals are available for the Hollywood Bowl (p66).
☎ 323-491-1300 ✉ 4th fl, Hollywood & Highland, 6801 Hollywood Blvd, Hollywood ⏲ 11:30am-10pm Mon-Fri, noon-10pm Sat & Sun 🚇 Hollywood/Highland 🅿 4hr validated $2 🚻

The sign of a true Hollywood landmark

WEST HOLLYWOOD

Ago (5, D4)
Tuscan $$$$
Overshadowing the dishy fare being cooked up in the elegant kitchen is the fact that Robert De Niro, Christopher Walken and Ridley Scott own an interest in this flirty New York–style joint. Don't accept a table in the small back room. Reservations advised.
☎ 323-655-6333
✉ 8478 Melrose Ave
🕑 noon-2:30pm Mon-Fri, 6-11:30pm Mon-Sat, 6-10pm Sun 🚌 DASH Fairfax ♿

Bastide (5, D4)
Eclectic $$$$
Chef Ludovic Lefebvre has made waves with his controversial, high-priced French fusion fare. Some are disappointed by the hype, or call the menu ridiculous; others find the haute experiment sublime. Reservations essential.
☎ 323-651-5950
✉ 8475 Melrose Pl 🕑 6-10pm Tue-Sat 🚌 MTA 10, 11

Greenblatt's Delicatessen (5, D2)
Jewish Deli $$
It's 'a wine shop that fronts as a deli,' and both parts are undeniably good. Tackle a triple-decker pastrami and matzo-ball soup, or pick up caviar and knishes to go.
☎ 323-656-0606 ✉ 8017 W Sunset Blvd 🕑 9am-2am 🚌 DASH Hollywood/West Hollywood Ⓟ 1hr free 🚹 Ⓥ

Griddle Café (5, E2)
American Breakfast $
This is where out-of-work actors hang when checking for casting calls from the next-door Directors Guild of America. Feed your hungry soul on high-octane coffee and comfort-food breakfasts. Warning: extreme sugar rushes are inevitable.
☎ 323-874-0377
✉ 7916 W Sunset Blvd
🕑 7am-3pm Mon-Fri, 8am-3pm Sat & Sun 🚌 DASH Hollywood/West Hollywood ♿ 🚹 Ⓥ

Koi (5, D4)
Japanese $$$$
Such A-listers as Madonna and Venus Williams have been spotted picking over plates of sushi, sashimi and black cod glazed with miso here. But come for the party, not the food. Bamboo-fringed patios, votive candles and a fireside lounge make the sexy scene. Reservations are advised.
☎ 310-659-9449 ✉ 730 N La Cienega Blvd 🕑 6-11pm Mon-Wed, 6-11:30pm Thu, 6pm-midnight Fri & Sat, 6-10pm Sun 🚌 MTA 105

Unearth a passion for all things organic at Urth Caffé

Pink's (5, F4)
American Fast Food $
Achieving cult status equally among celebs, struggling musicians and schoolkids, family-owned Pink's has been serving hot dogs since 1939. The long lines give you plenty of time to decide on which toppings you'd like.
☎ 323-931-4223 ✉ 709 N La Brea Ave 🕑 9:30am-2am Sun-Thu, 9:30am-3am Fri & Sat 🚌 MTA 212 ♿ 🚹

Urth Caffé (5, C4)
Healthy Californian $$
Nab a terrace table outside this eternally trendy spot, where everything is organic, right down to the fresh-roasted coffee beans and table linens. Tofu–brown rice wraps and 18-Carrot Gold cake are picks of the crop. You can find another Urth Caffé on Main St in Santa Monica (4, A3).
☎ 310-659-0628 ✉ 8565 Melrose Ave 🕑 6:30am-11:30pm 🚌 DASH Fairfax Ⓥ

MID-CITY

A.O.C. (5,D5)
Mediterranean Tapas $$$$
This hugely popular, celeb-happy hunting ground of the rich and lithe defines stylish. The small-plate menu will have you noshing on homemade charcuterie, rare cheeses and richly nuanced dishes such as braised pork confit with roasted plums. There are over 50 wines by the glass.
☎ 323-653-6359 ⊠ 8022 W 3rd St ⏲ 6-11pm Mon-Fri, 5:30-11pm Sat, 5:30-10pm Sun 🚌 MTA 16 Ⓥ

Campanile (5, F5)
Cal-French $$$
Occupying a spot in the city's culinary pantheon for over 15 years, chef-owner Mark Peel knows how to turn market-fresh ingredients into beautiful dishes that will linger in your memory long after you've left the dining room (inside Charlie Chaplin's offices). You'll need to make reservations.
☎ 323-938-1447 ⊠ 624 S La Brea Ave ⏲ 11:30am-2pm Mon-Fri, 9:30am-1:30pm Sat & Sun,

5:30-11pm Mon-Sat 🚌 MTA 212 ♿ Ⓥ

Canter's Delicatessen (5, E4)
Jewish Deli $
Plainly a neighborhood favorite, no-nonsense Canter's has sold over 10 million matzo balls since 1931. The service here is infamously brusque and it's busy around the clock, yet the fruit-flavored *rugelach* (cream-cheese pastry) sold by the bakery ladies is divine.
☎ 323-651-2030 ⊠ 419 N Fairfax Ave ⏲ 24hr 🚌 DASH Fairfax Ⓟ 2hr free ♿ 🚼 Ⓥ

Cobras & Matadors (5, E4)
Spanish Tapas $$
Tables at this tapas bar are crushed together like lovers, but scoring one can still be a tall order. A strong menu shows authentic Catalan and Basque touches. If you pick up a bottle of vino at the shop next door, you won't pay a corkage fee. Also in Los Feliz (5, G5).
☎ 323-932-6178 ⊠ 7615 W Beverly Blvd ⏲ 6-11pm Sun-Thu, 6pm-midnight Fri & Sat 🚌 MTA 14

Grace (5, F4)
New American $$$
The simple Asian-esque decor is deceptive, because complex culinary adventures await you here. Richly sauced steaks, delicate seafood and revolution-ary comfort food like the house-made doughnuts for dessert star on rebel chef Neal Fraser's menu.
☎ 323-934-4400 ⊠ 7360 Beverly Blvd ⏲ 5:30-11pm Tue-Thu, 5:30pm-midnight Fri & Sat, 5:30-10pm Sun 🚌 MTA 14 ♿

Original Farmers Market (5, E5)
International $
A touristy but tasty array of produce and seafood merchants, bakery-cafés and sandwich shops line up by the landmark 1940s clock tower. Worth trying are Du-par's Pies, Cajun-style cooking at the Gumbo Pot, ¡Loteria! Mexican grill and Singapore's Banana Leaf.
☎ 323-933-9211 ⊠ 6333 W 3rd St ⏲ 9am-9pm Mon-Fri, 9am-8pm Sat, 10am-7pm Sun 🚌 DASH Fairfax Ⓟ 2hr validated free ♿ 🚼 Ⓥ

NIGHT-OWL NOSHES
LA is a sanctuary for 24-hour and late-night eateries. Some are classic, some shock-ingly bad – but all have personality. Best bets are Fred 62 (p48), Canter's Delicatessen (above), Bob's Big Boy (p55) and these hang-outs:
Original Pantry Cafe (7, A5; ☎ 213-972-9279; 877 S Figueroa St, downtown LA) Owned by ex-mayor Richard Riordan, city movers and shakers and club kids chow down here. Cash only.
Swingers (Beverly Laurel Motor Hotel, p73) Sassy, short-skirted waitresses in fishnet stockings serve at this funky diner. Also in Santa Monica (4, B2).
The Standard (5, D2; ☎ 323-650-9090; 8300 W Sunset Blvd, West Hollywood) Futuristic coffee shop with ultra-hip clientele. Also downtown (p73).

BEVERLY HILLS

Chaya Brasserie (5, C4)
Eurasian $$$
Zen meets industrial chic inside this serene dining room. Appetizers such as the layered Dungeness crab and avocado literally reach for the stars, and vice-versa. Dress sharp, and book ahead or order at the happening bar. Also in Venice (4, A4).
☎ 310-859-8833
✉ 8741 Alden Dr
⌚ 11:30am-2:30pm Mon-Fri, 6-10:30pm Mon-Thu, 6-11pm Fri & Sat, 6-10pm Sun
🚌 DASH Fairfax ♿

Crustacean (5, A5)
Eurasian $$$$
At this clubby restaurant, you can literally walk on water – atop a floor-sunken koi stream. Top honors go to the whole roasted Dungeness crab and garlic noodles, bathed in owner-chef Elizabeth An's 'secret spices.' Reservations here are essential.
☎ 310-205-8990
✉ 9646 S Santa Monica Blvd
⌚ 11:30am-2:30pm Mon-Fri, 5:30-10pm Mon-Sat
🚌 MTA 16 ♿

Kate Mantilini (5, B5)
American Classic $$
Industry types graze at this snobby, but artful diner. The chef's healthy versions don't sacrifice the glorious guts of yesteryear dishes, such as a petite filet mignon sandwich and slice of lemon icebox pie.
☎ 310-278-3699
✉ 9101 Wilshire Blvd
⌚ 7:30am-midnight Mon, 7:30am-1am Tue-Thu, 7:30am-2am Fri, 11am-2am

Dine out with the stars at Spago

Sat, 10am-2am Sun
🚌 MTA 720 ♿ Ⓥ

Mako (5, B5)
Asian Fusion $$$
Be truly wowed at this minimalist-chic restaurant, where a small-plate menu is ideal for sampling flavors and textures. At lunch most people order the *bentō* (meal in a box), filled with whatever inspires champion chef Makoto Tanaka that day.
☎ 310-288-8338 ✉ 225 S Beverly Dr ⌚ noon-2pm Wed-Fri, 6-10pm Mon-Sat
🚌 MTA 720 ♿

Nate 'n Al's (5, A5)
Jewish Deli $-$$
It's not much to look at, but this landmark makes quite possibly the best lox on bagels this side of Manhattan.

If you're lucky, you'll spot a star chowing down here, too.
☎ 310-274-0101 ✉ 414 N Beverly Dr ⌚ 7am-9pm
🚌 MTA 714 ♿ ♿ Ⓥ

Spago (5, B5)
Cal-Italian $$$$
Wolfgang Puck's flagship emporium has long been tops for celebrity-spotting. Score a table on the garden patio and prepare your taste buds to do cartwheels as chef Lee Hefter gives Sonoma lamb and mascarpone agnolotti the gourmet treatment. Reservations essential.
☎ 310-385-0880 ✉ 176 N Cañon Dr ⌚ 11:30am-2:15pm Mon-Fri, noon-2:30pm Sat, 5:30-10pm Sun-Thu, 5:30-11pm Fri & Sat
🚌 MTA 720 ♿ Ⓥ

TIP-TOP VIEWS
For city skyline views, **Windows** (7, A5; ☎ 213-746-1554; 32nd fl, Transamerica Bldg, 1150 S Olive St, downtown) serves respectable steaks and martinis. Barney Greengrass (p39) is a beautiful rooftop oasis in Beverly Hills. Hollywood's Yamashiro (p58) is an uplifting place just for drinks, as is the *Jetsons*-style Encounter Restaurant at LAX airport (p83).

SANTA MONICA

Border Grill (4, A2)
Cal-Mexican $$-$$$
Run by the same chefs as downtown's Ciudad (p46), this is the original branch of an expanding empire. From grilled skirt steaks to plantain empanadas, there's always a touchy of whimsy. Reservations recommended.
☎ 310-451-1655 ✉ 1445 4th St ◷ 11:30am-10pm Sun-Thu, 11:30am-11pm Fri & Sat 🚍 BBB 1, 2, 3, 4, 7 ♿ ♨ Ⓥ

Father's Office (4, B1)
Burger Bar $$
With over 40 quality microbrews on hand, this retro resto-bar is famous for its hamburgers slathered with blue cheese, applewood-

smoked bacon and caramelized onions. For grazers, there's an array of tapas.
☎ 310-393-2337 ✉ 1018 Montana Ave ◷ 5-10pm Mon-Wed, 5-11pm Thu, 4-11pm Fri, 3-11pm Sat, 3-10pm Sun, bar open later 🚍 BBB 3 ♿

JiRaffe (4, A2)
Cal-French $$$
An avid surfer, owner-chef Raphael Lunetta learned his craft in Paris and now regales diners with his signature roast-beet salad and other flavor-intensive dishes. The walnut furniture and original art give the dining room a private-mansion feel.
☎ 310-917-6671 ✉ 502 Santa Monica Blvd ◷ 6-9pm Mon, 6-10pm Tue-Thu,

6-11pm Fri & Sat, 5:30-9pm Sun 🚍 BBB 1 ♿

Mélisse (4, B2)
Contemporary French $$$$
Mélisse wows a Rolls-Royce crowd of diners with Oscar-worthy food and an elegant dining room. Owner-chef Josiah Citrin imagines market-fresh palate teasers such as sweet white-corn ravioli with smoked bacon and truffle froth. Exquisite cheese tray.
☎ 310-395-0881 ✉ 1104 Wilshire Blvd ◷ 6-9:30pm Tue-Thu, 6-10pm Fri & Sat 🚍 BBB 2 ♿

Real Food Daily (4, A2)
Healthy Vegetarian $
Tempted by tempeh? Salivating for seitan? Vegan cooking queen Ann Gentry gives you the gourmet treatment. Start off with lentil-walnut paté, then finish with a rich tofu cheesecake with fruit topping. There's a kosher branch in West Hollywood (5, D4).
☎ 310-451-7544 ✉ 514 Santa Monica Blvd ◷ 11:30am-10pm 🚍 BBB 1 ♿ ♨ Ⓥ

The Lobster (4, A2)
Seafood $$$
You're by the ocean, so seafood it is. While a simple, sweet lobster can be surprisingly hard to find along the coast, here ex–Water Grill (p47) chef Allyson Thurber makes it de rigueur. At sunset, reserve a table on the glass-enclosed deck.
☎ 310-458-9294 ✉ 1602 Ocean Ave ◷ 11:30am-10pm Sun-Thu, 11:30am-11pm Fri & Sat 🚍 Tide Shuttle, BBB 1 ♿ ♨

There's room for a giraffe at JiRaffe's

VENICE

Abbot's Pizza (4, A5)
Californian/Take-Out $
Join the leagues of surfers, students and urbanites at this little walk-in joint for its addictive bagel-crust pizzas. Go gourmet, with maybe a slice of barbecue chicken or olive pesto.
☎ 310-396-7334
✉ 1407 Abbot Kinney Blvd
☼ 11am-11pm 🚌 BBB 3
♿ ♨ **V**

Hal's Bar & Grill (4, A4)
New American $$$
Hal's cool industrial loft is brightened by revolving artwork. Matched with an elaborate wine list, the menu changes seasonally but always features solid fare: no fusion, no apologies. Live jazz on Sunday and Monday nights.
☎ 310-396-3105
✉ 1349 Abbot Kinney Blvd
☼ 11:30am-2am Mon-Fri, 11am-2am Sat & Sun
🚌 BBB 3 ♿ **V**

Jody Maroni's Sausage Kingdom (4, A5)
Californian/Take-Out $
Even picky eaters will be pleased by these plump all-natural 'haut dogs.' If you can't make up your mind between hot Italian with oranges and fennel or lime-laced tequila chicken, ask

Jazz things up at Hal's Bar & Grill

for free, hot samples. Also at Universal City Walk (p10).
☎ 310-822-5639
✉ 2011 Ocean Front Walk
☼ 10am-sunset, weather permitting 🚌 BBB 1
♿ ♨

Joe's (4, A4)
Cal-French $$$
Owner-chef Joe Miller has built this neighborhood eatery into a charmingly unpretentious destination, so book ahead. His sophisticated seasonal menu is anything but basic, with prix-fixe lunch deals and eclectic tasting menus. Romantics take back-patio tables.
☎ 310-399-5811 ✉ 1023 Abbot Kinney Blvd ☼ noon-2:30pm Tue-Fri, 11am-2:30pm Sat & Sun, 6-10pm

Sun & Tue-Thu, 6-11pm Fri & Sat 🚌 BBB 3 **V**

Piccolo (4, A4)
Italian $$-$$$
This teensy spot, mere steps from the sand, pays homage to the 'real' Venice. The gracious proprietors hail straight from Italy, and they shower patrons with handmade pastas, daringly flavor-packed meats and delightful desserts.
☎ 310-314-3222
✉ 5 Dudley Ave
☼ 5:30-10pm Mon-Thu, 5-11pm Fri & Sat, 5-10pm Sun 🚌 BBB 2 **V**

Venice Cantina (4, A4)
Cal-Mexican $$
Inside a century-old hotel adorned with Mexican ceramic tiles, nightlife gurus have brought a hip flavor to the Venice boardwalk. Fresh seafood and heavy traditional sauces are served at beachside tables perfect for people-watching.
☎ 310-399-8420 ✉ 23 Windward Ave ☼ 4-10pm Mon-Fri, 11am-11pm Sat & Sun 🚌 BBB 2 **V**

GOOD GREENS
Almost every LA restaurant knows to provide at least a few menu options for vegetarians (and vegans). Look for the **V** icon after reviews of exceptionally vegetarian-friendly eateries. Standouts include Urth Caffé (p49), Real Food Daily (opposite), Spot (p54) and Inn of the Seventh Ray (p54).

SOUTH BAY

Avenue (3, B4)
New American $$$
This earth-toned bistro is just one of Manhattan Beach's grown-up destinations for haute cuisine. Farm-fresh dishes, like feta-crusted lamb chops with roasted tomato soup, are always inventive, as is the wine list. Reservations recommended.
☎ 310-802-1973 ✉ 1141 Manhattan Ave, Manhattan Beach ☾ 10:30am-2:30pm Sat & Sun, 5:30-10pm Sun-Thu, 5:30-11pm Fri & Sat 🚌 MTA 439

Bluewater Grill (3, C4)
Seafood $$$
A beautiful view of the marina and seafood that couldn't be more fresh, from Minnesota walleye to Fijian ahi to Costa Rican mahimahi, plus all the warm, sourdough bread you can eat.
☎ 310-318-3474 ✉ 665 N Harbor Dr, Redondo Beach ☾ 11:30am-10pm Mon-Thu, 11:30am-11pm Fri & Sat, 10am-10pm Sun 🚌 MTA 439 ♿ ♿

Full to the gills at Uncle Bill's

Spot (3, C4)
International Vegetarian $
This stalwart of healthy eating cooks up topflight vegan and vegetarian food in an unpretentious setting. A back-to-basics menu also includes more fanciful mushroom-walnut loaf. Portions are big.
☎ 310-376-2355 ✉ 110 2nd St, Hermosa Beach ☾ 11am-10pm 🚌 MTA 130, 439 ♿ Ⓥ

Uncle Bill's Pancake House (3, B4)
American Breakfast $
Long weekend lines wrap around this landmark, where ocean-view deck tables are prized, especially by surfers. Choose from a cornucopia of pancake toppings, crunchy waffles with savory or sweet fillings, and fresh omelettes.
☎ 310-545-5177 ✉ 1305 Highland Ave, Manhattan Beach ☾ 6am-3pm Mon-Fri, 7am-3pm Sat & Sun 🚌 MTA 126, 439 ♿ Ⓥ

MALIBU & BEYOND

The celebrity factor is high in Malibu, including at star-chef establishments like **Nobu** (3, A3; ☎ 310-317-9140; Malibu Country Mart, 3835 Crosscreek Rd) and Wolfgang Puck's **Granita** (3, A3; ☎ 310-456-0488; Malibu Colony Plaza, 23725 W Malibu Rd).

Inn of the Seventh Ray (3, A2)
Healthy Californian $$$
Philosophy, not just cooking, is served at this karmically aligned place. It's an idyllic mountain retreat with fountain courtyard tables, where organic produce, local seafood, and free-range chickens and eggs are on the menu. Like a ray of sunshine, service here is all smiles. Reservations are preferred.
☎ 310-455-1311 ✉ 128 Old Topanga Canyon Rd, Topanga ☾ 11:30am-3pm Mon-Fri, 10:30am-3pm Sat, 9:30am-3pm Sun, 5:30-10pm daily ♿ Ⓥ

Moonshadows (3, A3)
Californian/Seafood $$$
Make no mistake: you are here for the prime view, not the service. With outdoor tables right above the crashing surf, this beautiful coastal hideaway is best visited at lunch (the cornmeal-fried oysters and cumin-crusted chicken are great) or for cocktails and a quick nosh at sunset.
☎ 310-456-3010 ✉ 20356 Pacific Coast Hwy (Hwy 1), Malibu ☾ 11:30am-10:30pm Sun-Thu, 11:30am-11pm Fri & Sat 🚌 MTA 434 ♿

Saddle Peak Lodge (3, A2)
Steakhouse $$$$
This award-winner may be remote, but carnivores will find it worth the drive for elk, venison, buffalo and other game in a setting watched over by mounted versions of the same. Reservations are recommended; dress well.
☎ 818-222-3888 ✉ 419 Cold Canyon Rd, off Piuma Rd, Calabasas ☾ 6-9pm Wed & Thu, 6-9:30pm Fri, 5-9:30pm Sat, 11am-1:30pm & 6-9pm Sun ♿

BURBANK & STUDIO CITY

Bob's Big Boy (6, B1)
American Classic $
For a genuine slice of Americana (or apple pie, for that matter), swing by this landmark coffee shop. On Friday and Sunday nights, the car-hop service catches that *American Graffiti* vibe; Friday is also classic-car night.
☎ 818-843-9334
✉ 4211 Riverside Dr at Rose St, Burbank ⏰ 24hr
🚍 MTA 152 ♿ 🅰

Sushi Nozawa (6, A2)
Japanese $$$$
Legend has it, the strict sushi chef once booted out someone who asked for a California roll. Amen, because that's the way fresh-fish aficionados like it. Expect to spend easily over $60 per head. No reservations, so get here when the doors open.
☎ 818-508-7017
✉ 11288 Ventura Blvd, east of Tujunga Ave, Studio City ⏰ noon-2pm & 5:30-10pm Mon-Fri 🚍 MTA 150

PASADENA

Bar Celona (1, B2)
Spanish Tapas $$
The mustard and rioja-tinted walls offer a fiery backdrop at this classy bar. Know your way around the tapas menu,

Hey there Big Boy!

or dig into big platters of paella and braised lamb.
☎ 626-405-1000
✉ 46 E Colorado Blvd
⏰ 11am-10pm Sun-Wed, 11am-11pm Thu, 11am-1:30am Fri & Sat
Ⓜ Memorial Park ♿ Ⓥ

Xiomara (1, B2)
Cuban/Latin $$$
Right on Pasadena's gourmet block, Xiomara's

spicy flavors will burst onto your plate as you imbibe a signature *mojito* (or two) at this humming Nuevo Latino bistro. They also run nearby casual Cafe Atlantic (1, B2) as well as Xiomara Hollywood (5, G4).
☎ 626-796-2520
✉ 69 N Raymond Ave
⏰ 11:30am-11pm Mon-Fri, 5-11pm Sat & Sun
Ⓜ Memorial Park ♿

LOOKS LIKE...

Of all the wacky roadside architecture in SoCal, almost nothing is as memorable as LA's mimetic fast-food stands. Near Beverly Center, visit **Tail O' the Pup** (5, C4; ☎ 310-652-4517; 329 N San Vicente Blvd, West Hollywood) for hot dogs, or 24-hour **Randy's Donuts** (3, C3; ☎ 310-645-4707; 805 W Manchester Ave, Inglewood) out by LAX. In the far eastern suburbs, **The Donut Hole** (3, E3; ☎ 626-968-2912; 15300 E Amar Rd, La Puente) drive-thru is shaped just like its namesake goodie.

Entertainment

LA is the entertainment-making capital of the USA. After-dark spots often overshadow and outnumber daytime diversions. Tomorrow's stars cut their teeth in today's comedy clubs and theaters. You can drop in at Marilyn Monroe's old watering hole in Hollywood, rock out on the Sunset Strip and see a film at a glittering movie palace, all within a few square miles.

LA also has plenty for fans of highbrow pursuits, including a world-class philharmonic orchestra and an opera led by Plácido Domingo. Year-round professional sports command a passionate following, too.

To put your finger on the city's pulse, check out the free **LA Weekly** (www.laweekly.com), free e-newsletter **Flavorpill LA** (http://la.flavorpill .net) or **Calendar Live** (www.calendarlive.com) in Sunday's *Los Angeles Times*. The city's **Cultural Affairs Department** (www.culturela.org) knows about festivals and special events going on around town; many of them are free.

Tickets for most concerts and sports events are sold at individual venues' box offices, as well as through ticketing agencies, which charge a booking fee of a few dollars. Contact **Ticketmaster** (☎ 213-480-3232; www .ticketmaster.com) or **TicketWeb** (☎ 866-777-8932; www.ticketweb.com). There are ticket outlets in Amoeba Music (p42), Tower Records and Wherehouse Music, as well as major department stores such as Robinsons-May and Macy's.

Half-price theater tickets for same-day evening shows and next-day matinees are sold at many box offices, at discount ticket agencies in Hollywood and online via the **LA Stage Alliance** (www.theatrela.org). A few theaters sell discounted 'rush tickets' to seniors and students with valid ID (or sometimes anyone at all) up to a few hours before performances start. Ticketmaster's **Fine Arts Line** (☎ 213-365-3500) sells full-price seats, plus a handling fee.

Smoking is banned in public places, and that includes bars and clubs. The ban is not always strictly enforced, however. Be careful driving at night, especially on weekends, as the hazard of drunk drivers is all too real.

It's a long way to the top when you wanna rock 'n' roll

SPECIAL EVENTS

Check with the LACVB (p91) for more information on current events.

January *Tournament of Roses* – around New Year's; flower-festooned floats along Pasadena's Colorado Blvd and at the Rose Bowl (p68) football game

Chinese New Year – late January/early February; century-old Golden Dragon Parade, fireworks and street fairs

February *Pan African Film & Arts Festival* – held during Black History Month

March *Academy Awards* – stars stroll up the Kodak Theatre's red carpet in Hollywood

LA Marathon – 26.2-mile race out to the Pacific Ocean and back; free entertainment

Blessing of the Animals – Saturday before Easter; in El Pueblo de Los Angeles

April *Toyota Grand Prix of Long Beach* – 2nd weekend; world-class auto racing

LA Times Festival of Books – late April; authors, writing workshops and storytelling, UCLA

Fiesta Broadway – last Sunday; largest Latino and Hispanic heritage festival in the USA

May *Venice Art Walk* – mid-May; tours of artists' studios, an art auction and food fair

Cinco de Mayo – May 5; Mexican festivities held around Olvera St in downtown LA

Topanga Banjo Fiddle Contest & Folk Festival – mid-May; bluegrass music, Paramount Ranch

June *LA Film Festival* – mid-June; indie shorts, world documentaries and features

Mariachi USA Festival – 3rd weekend; mariachi music and ballet *folklórico,* Hollywood Bowl

LA Pride – late June; gay and lesbian parade on Santa Monica Blvd, concerts and parties galore in West Hollywood

July *Grand Performances* – July to September; free world performing arts at California Plaza, downtown LA

Twilight Dance Series – Thursday evenings July to August; pop, swing, zydeco and reggae concerts, Santa Monica Pier

4th of July – Independence Day fireworks, LA Philharmonic concert at the Hollywood Bowl

Lotus Festival – weekend after July 4; celebrates Asian and Pacific Islander culture with dragon-boat races, food and fireworks

Orange County Fair – livestock exhibits, carnival rides and live entertainment, Costa Mesa

Festival of Arts – July and August; art exhibitions, 'Pageant of the Masters' living tableaus, Laguna Beach

August *International Surf Festival* – early August; lifeguards, bodysurfing, sand castles and more, South Bay

Nisei Week Japanese Festival – early to mid-August; *taiko* drumming, tofu eating and dancing, Little Tokyo

Long Beach Jazz Festival – mid-August; world-class jazz performed near a lagoon

Sunset Junction Street Fair – late August; multi-block multicultural street fest, Silver Lake

African Marketplace & Cultural Faire – late August to early September; celebrates the African diaspora, Exposition Park

September *Watts Towers Day of the Drum & Jazz Festivals* – late September; free jazz, gospel, blues and drumming

October *West Hollywood Halloween Carnival* – October 31; wild street fair on Santa Monica Blvd

November *Dia de Los Muertos* – November 2; Mexican 'Day of the Dead' festival, Olvera St

Doo Dah Parade (p29)

December *Christmas* – month-long celebrations include Griffith Park's Light Festival, Hollywood Christmas Parade, Olvera St candlelight processions and holiday boat parades

BARS

Bars usually open in the late afternoon, but some unlock their doors before noon. Closing time is around 2am. Some of the beach towns' eateries (p52) also have vivacious bars. For live-music hot spots, see p62.

Hanging for some good luck? Good Luck Bar (opposite)

Aloha Sharkeez (3, C4)
It's always fiesta time at this 'Animal House by the sea,' where potent libations and an abundance of bare skin help fan the party zone. Its spit-and-sawdust sister cantina is **Baja Sharkeez** (3, B4; ☎ 310-545-6563; 3801 Highland Ave, Manhattan Beach).
☎ 310-374-7823 ✉ 52 Pier Ave at Hermosa Ave, Hermosa Beach ◔ 11am-2am Mon-Fri, 9am-2am Sat & Sun 🚌 MTA 130, 439

Beauty Bar (5, C1)
At this pint-sized cocktail bar, decorated with hair-salon paraphernalia from the Kennedy era, you can scan the preening crowd from vintage swivel chairs beneath plastic hair dryers. Manicure-and-martini happy hours are as fabulous as nearby **Star Shoes** (5, C1; ☎ 323-462-7827; 6364 Hollywood Blvd, Hollywood), a DJ lounge that sells vintage shoes.
☎ 323-464-7676 ✉ 1638 N Cahuenga Blvd, Hollywood ◔ 9pm-2am Sun-Wed, 6pm-2am Thu-Sat ◉ Hollywood/Vine

Bigfoot Lodge (6, F3)
Smokey the Bear presides over this laid-back log cabin setting, a cool spot to camp out for a drink or two (try the minty Girl Scout Cookie). The action at Bigfoot Lodge starts to heat up when there's live Brit-pop bands, kamikaze karaoke (they pick the song, then you sing it) or retro DJs hitting the decks.
☎ 323-662-9227 ✉ 3172 Los Feliz Blvd, Los Feliz ◔ 5pm-2am 🚌 MTA 180, 181 ♿

Daddy's (5, D1)
A low-lit lounge with sensuously curved booths (and hips), Daddy's got the same killer mixed jukebox as its sexy Silver Lake sister, the circular **4100 Bar** (5, H6; ☎ 323-666-4460; 4100 W Sunset Blvd).
☎ 323-463-7777 ✉ 1610 N Vine St, Hollywood ◔ 7pm-2am Fri, 8pm-2am Sat-Thu ◉ Hollywood/Vine

TINSELTOWN TIPPLIN'
Back in Hollywood's Golden Age, every star had their favorite dive. Follow in the footsteps of Marilyn Monroe and Humphry Bogart to **Formosa Cafe** (5, F3; ☎ 323-850-9050; 7156 Santa Monica Blvd). Ed Wood frequented **Boardner's** (5, B1; ☎ 323-462-9621; 1652 N Cherokee Ave). During WWII Bette Davis entertained the troops at **Hollywood Canteen** (5, G3; ☎ 323-465-0961; 1006 Seward St), with its Airstream trailer. At Musso & Frank Grill (p48), Charlie Chaplin knocked back gimlets at the bar. High up in the hills, **Yamashiro** (5, F2; ☎ 323-466-5125; 1999 N Sycamore Ave) is a faux-Japanese castle where silent-screen stars once hobnobbed.

HIP HOTEL BARS

For big heapings of eye candy and A-list celebs, call ahead or line up early behind the velvet rope at:

Bar Marmont (p70) A chill-out spot for stars at Chateau Marmont.

Cameo (p71) Ultrachic oceanfront cabanas at Viceroy.

Polo Lounge (p70) Starlets and Industry movers 'n' shakers at the Beverly Hills Hotel.

Rooftop Bar (below) Downtown LA is heating up, literally.

Skybar (5, D3; ☎ 323-848-6025; Mondrian, 8440 W Sunset Blvd, West Hollywood) Hoochie mamas with attitude and altitude.

Tropicana (p72) Hollywood glamour poolside at the Roosevelt Hotel.

Whiskey Blue (☎ 310-443-8232; W Hotel, 930 Hilgard Ave, Westwood) Sexy sorority sisters, and more.

Good Luck Bar (5, H5)
Decked out like a fantasy Chinese opium den, the paper lanterns at this cultish watering hole cast a siren's red glow. The clientele is cool, the jukebox loud and the drinks seductively strong. Be sure to pick up a matchbook.
☎ 323-666-3524 ⊠ 1514 Hillhurst Ave, Silver Lake ⏰ 7pm-2am Mon-Thu, 8pm-2am Fri & Sat 🚌 MTA 2

Mountain Bar (7, C3)
Poets and hipsters gather at this artsy Chinatown bar for a nightcap after gallery hopping on nearby Chung King Rd. The Kool Aid–orange decor makes you feel like you're sitting inside a volcano.
☎ 213-625-7500 ⊠ 473 Gin Ling Way, Chinatown ⏰ 6pm-2am Tue-Sun ⊕ Chinatown ♿

Otheroom (4, A4)
A sceney sister to Manhattan's original sleek hangout, this microbrew and wine bar is Venice, but all grown up. Grab a candlelit table, or, on airy nights, a velvet-lined window-side bench. The groove all

depends on the whims of the bartender's iPod.
☎ 310-396-6230 ⊠ 1201 Abbot Kinney Blvd, Venice ⏰ 5pm-2am 🚌 BBB 2 ♿

Rooftop Bar (7, B4)
This outdoor lounge, swimming in a sea of skyscrapers, is libidinous, intense and more than a bit surreal. There are vibrating waterbed pods for lounging, hot-bod servers and a pool for when it gets too steamy. Velvet rope on weekends.
☎ 213-892-8080 ⊠ The Standard, 550 S Flower St, downtown LA 💲 after 7pm Fri-Sun $20 ⏰ noon-1:30am ⊕ 7th St/Metro Center

Tiki Ti (5, H6)
The trick is finding out for sure when this legendary hole-in-the-wall actually opens, since the owners go surfing a lot. There's a wicked collection of tropical kitsch, a bamboo bar and vintage mixologists on hand to please. Only cash is accepted.
☎ 323-669-9381 ⊠ 4427 W Sunset Blvd, Silver Lake ⏰ usually 6pm-12:30am Wed-Sun 🚌 MTA 2, 4

DANCE CLUBS

To confirm all the LA clichés, look no further than Hollywood's Cahuenga Corridor clubs. Come armed with a hot bod or a fat wallet to get past the velvet rope, especially on weekends. Showing up early can help you avoid long lines and cover charges – maybe.

Arena/Circus (5, G3)
Club Spundae, a weekly mega–dance club event, draws trance, progressive and house DJs and dance devotees of all sexual orientations. It's unmistakably a gay boy's disco on Tuesdays, though. Other nights you'll hear live Latin grooves or hip-hop. The warehouse-sized space is huge, with three dance floors and a starlight deck.
☎ 323-462-0714 ⊠ 6655 Santa Monica Blvd, West Hollywood 💲 $3-20 ⏰ 9pm-2am Tue-Thu & Sun, 9pm-4am Fri & Sat 🚌 MTA 4, 156

Club Mayan (7, B5)
If you crave a little salsa and merengue, or want to hear

Cocktails, with a dash of feng shui, White Lotus

DJs spin some Latin house, step up to the Mayan Theatre, a 1927 movie palace designed in pre–Columbian Revival style. Extremely strict dress codes can't stop *la vida loca*.
☎ 213-746-4674 🖳 www.clubmayan.com ✉ 1038 S Hill St, downtown LA
💲 $8-15 🕑 9pm-3am Fri & Sat 🚌 MTA 2, 4

Derby (3, C2)
Long after the craze inspired by the movie *Swingers* died down, the pint-sized dance floor still throbs with weekly jump jive, swing and rockabilly nights, and now even burlesque.
☎ 323-663-8979
🖳 www.the-derby.com
✉ 4500 Los Feliz Blvd, Los Feliz 💲 $5-10 🕑 schedule varies 🚌 MTA 180, 181

Garden of Eden (5, A1)
No, it's not a nudist club, but there's certainly no shortage of skin-baring temptresses at this fashionable hip-hop haven. This exotic double-decker venue attracts its share of A-list athletic royalty. Dress to impress, or just fuhgeddaboutit.
☎ 323-465-3336
🖳 www.gardenofedenla.com
✉ 7080 Hollywood Blvd, Hollywood 💲 $20
🕑 10pm-2am Fri-Sun
🚌 MTA 717

King King (5, C1)
In the heart of Hollywood yet far removed from the glam circuit, excellent local talent holds forth in a lofty industrial-chic warehouse with a bar on wheels. Salsa and no-cover rock on weeknights make way for weekend house DJs.
☎ 323-960-9234 ✉ 6655 Hollywood Blvd, Hollywood
💲 free-$20 🕑 9pm-2am Tues-Thu, 9pm-4am Fri & Sat
🚌 MTA 217

Little Temple (5, H6)
An Eastside cousin to Santa Monica's cross-cultural Temple Bar (4, B2), this DJ lounge is perfect for anyone with a yen for Zen, from soulful sounds and blissed-out beats to new hip-hop stylin' and reggaeton.
☎ 323-660-4540
🖳 www.littletemple.com
✉ 4519 Santa Monica Blvd, Silver Lake
💲 $5-10 🕑 closed Mon
🚇 Vermont/Santa Monica

White Lotus (5, C1)
At the peak of the Cahuenga Corridor, sizzling White Lotus is a stylish restaurant-club combo – done up feng shui–style – perfect if you're not into switching venues halfway through a night of partying. Access to the dance floor mobbed with paparazzi-pretty people is guaranteed with dinner reservations. Also at **Cabana** (5, G2; ☎ 323-463-0005; 1439 Ivar Ave), next to Sterling Steakhouse.
☎ 323-463-0060 🖳 www.whitelotushollywood.com
✉ 1743 N Cahuenga Blvd, Hollywood 💲 $10-20
🕑 9pm-2am Tue-Sat
🚇 Hollywood/Vine

Zanzibar (4, A2)
KCRW (89.9FM) radio spinmeisters Jason Bentley and Garth Trinidad work their turntable magic on throngs of beat fanatics at this hot boîte with sensuous African decor. The wraparound bar is ace for socializing, while comfy couches invite intimacy.
☎ 310-451-2221
🖳 www.zanzibarlive.com
✉ 1301 5th St, Santa Monica
💲 $5-10 🕑 9pm-2am Tue-Sun 🚌 BBB 5

COMEDY CLUBS

Most comedy clubs are adults-only and have limited seating capacity, so it's best to call ahead and make reservations. Expect a two-drink minimum, plus the cover charge.

Acme Comedy Theatre (5, F4)

Bone-tickling funny men and women rage at this totally entertaining space, with sketch comedy from screenwriters, B-list actors and students of the on-site comedy school. Thursdays are for improv jams.
☎ 323-525-0202 ✉ 135 N La Brea Ave, Mid-City $ $15 ⏱ shows Wed-Sun 🚌 MTA 212 ♿

Comedy & Magic Club (3, C4)

Sometimes Jay Leno fine-tunes his jokes here on Sunday nights. Headliners like Chris Rock and George Carlin do stand-up at this Vegas-style club near the beach, which also has a few magicians on hand.
☎ 310-372-1193 🖥 www .comedyandmagicclub.info ✉ 1018 Hermosa Ave, Hermosa Beach $ $12-25

You've got to be joking...well, these guys are, anyway

(2-drink min) ⏱ closed Mon 🚌 MTA 130, 439 ♿

Comedy Store (5, D3)

Remember the Playboy Channel's *Girls of the Comedy Store*? You can thank the owner Mitzi Shore, mother of comedian Pauly, who transformed this first-rate comedy club, now with its own reality-TV series. There's often no cover charge for the upstairs Belly Room.
☎ 323-650-6268 🖥 www.thecomedystore .com ✉ 8433 W Sunset Blvd, West Hollywood $ $5-20 (2-drink min) ⏱ shows nightly 🚌 MTA 2, 302

Groundlings (5, F4)

The inimitable Groundlings comedy troupe conjure up the funny every night, whether it's sketch or improv. Surprise celebs and alums who've gone on to *Saturday Night Live* and *Mad TV* often drop by Thursday nights.
☎ 323-934-4747 🖥 www.groundlings.com ✉ 7307 Melrose Ave, West Hollywood $ $10-20 ⏱ shows nightly 🚌 MTA 10, 11 ♿ 👶

Laugh Factory (5, D2)

Comedians Jerry Seinfeld and Ellen DeGeneres have done stand-up at this Sunset Strip castle built in 1979. Attitudinous staff and around-the-block lines are offset by hand-picked talent. The best nights are Chocolate Sundaes and Latino Mondays.
☎ 323-656-1336 🖥 www.laughfactory.com ✉ 8001 W Sunset Blvd, West Hollywood $ $15-20 (2-drink min) ⏱ shows nightly 🚌 MTA 2, 302

SOLO ANGELS

LA ain't an easy town for singles. Even at many coffee-houses (p62), people are intent on pecking out screenplays on their laptops, not striking up a conversation. And then there's that ego-destroying LA stare, where you're put under the fashion microscope to see if you're A-list material. But don't despair yet. To meet fascinating, but not-too-famous Angelenos, hit the beaches (p16), work out at a gym (p87), visit a spa (p28), drop by a museum (p20) or skim the events calendars in the *LA Weekly* (p90).

LIVE MUSIC

At smaller venues, you can generally walk right in after paying the cover charge, especially midweek, though it depends on who's playing. For headliner shows, buy tickets in advance. Call the clubs' box offices directly for more information. For free live shows, try LA's coffeehouses (see below).

Catalina Bar & Grill (5, G2)
LA's smoothest jazz club has moved into new, slicker and more spacious digs. Lots of jazz greats have graced Catalina's stage over the years, from Dizzy Gillespie to Art Blakey to the Marsalis brothers.
☎ 323-466-2210 ⌨ www.catalinajazzclub.com ✉ 6725 W Sunset Blvd, Hollywood ⓢ $10-35 (2-drink min) ☽ closed Mon ⊕ Hollywood/Highland ♿

Conga Room (5, F6)
Jennifer Lopez co-owns this spacious Latin nightclub, with the decadent feel of

prerevolution Havana (upscale attire is required). Salsa orchestras are first-rate and Latin jazz greats appear with amazing regularity. Come early for salsa lessons, or buy tickets in advance.
☎ 323-938-1696 ⌨ www.congaroom.com ✉ 5364 Wilshire Blvd, Mid-City ⓢ $10-50 ☽ 9pm-1:30am Thu & Fri, 8pm-2am Sat ⨋ MTA 720 ♿

Harvelle's (4, A2)
The Chicago vibe at this swank blues joint is so real. Harvelle's has been packing 'em in since 1931. There are no big-name acts here by the beach, but baby, it's quality all the way.
☎ 310-395-1676 ⌨ www.harvelles.com ✉ 1432 4th St, Santa Monica ⓢ $5-10 ☽ shows nightly ⨋ BBB 1, 2, 3, 4, 7 ♿

Hotel Café (5, C1)
The friendliest respite in the hot Cahuenga Corridor, this tiny coffeehouse (yes, they also serve food and a few drinks) is at the epicenter of LA's folk and acoustic scene.

Show up early to score a table.
☎ 323-461-2040 ⌨ www.hotelcafe.com ✉ 1623½ N Cahuenga Blvd, Hollywood ⓢ $5-10 ☽ shows almost nightly ⊕ Hollywood/Vine ♿

House of Blues (5, D3)
This premier chain venue that looks like a Mississippi Delta shack helped revive the Sunset Strip in the '90s. Come for top-quality acts (Etta James to Australian rock, West Coast hip-hop to Beck), even though there are no actual seats. Also at Universal City (p10) and Disneyland (p9).
☎ 323-848-5100 ⌨ www.hob.com ✉ 8430 Sunset Blvd, West Hollywood ⓢ shows $15-35, brunch $33/17 ☽ shows Mon-Sat, gospel brunch 10am & 1pm Sun ⨋ MTA 2 ♿

Knitting Factory (5, A1)
This bastion of indie bands isn't as out there as the New York City mother club, but there's still incredible world music, progressive jazz and other indie sounds. The inti-

JONESIN' FOR JAVA
Most of LA's cool indie coffeehouses are off the beaten track.
Hidden downtown in El Pueblo (p18), **Xococafé** (7, C4; 19 Olvera St) serves an aphrodisiac of Mexican hot chocolate with espresso from behind a mosaic-tiled bar.
At Venice Beach is sunshine-filled **Cow's End** (4, A5; ☎ 310-574-1080; 34 Washington Blvd), while inland **Anastasia's Asylum** (4, B2; ☎ 310-394-7113; 1028 Wilshire Blvd, Santa Monica) is a dark boudoir-style haunt. Both have live-music shows some nights.
Melrose Ave's Urth Caffé (p49) has another branch in Santa Monica (4, A3). Up in Hollywood, the **Green Room** (5, B1; ☎ 323-860-0775; 6752 Hollywood Blvd) has outdoor tables with cool tunes drifting over from the next-door Musicians Institute.
South of Hollywood, **Highland Grounds** (5, F4; ☎ 323-466-1507; 742 N Highland Ave) is a beatnik enclave with a full bar and live music on weekends. East in bohemian Silver Lake, **Casbah Café** (5, H6; ☎ 323-664-7000; 3900 W Sunset Blvd) has a French colonial vibe and wickedly rich coffee.

The Whisky opened doors for The Doors

mate AlterKnit Lounge is often free. Some all-ages shows.
☎ 323-463-0204
🖳 www.knittingfactory.com
✉ 7021 Hollywood Blvd, Hollywood $ around $10
☽ shows nightly
⊕ Hollywood/Highland

McCabe's Guitar Shop (4, C3)
Fans of folk, bluegrass, roots and alt-acoustic make their way to this no-frills store-front, where everyone from Lucinda Williams to G Love has played. The seats are back-killers and sight lines are blocked, but who cares when the space is so wonder-fully warm? No alcohol, but there's free coffee.
☎ 310-828-4497
🖳 www.mccabes.com
✉ 3101 W Pico Blvd at 31st St, Santa Monica ☽ shows Fri-Sun $ tickets $15-20
🚍 BBB 7 ♿ ⚤

Roxy (5, C3)
A Sunset Blvd fixture since 1973, the Roxy is a launch pad for rock bands on the verge of stardom. The club prides itself on a 'no bullshit factor' and draws a diverse crowd, from the multi-pierced to short-skirted. Last-minute gigs by famous faces happen here. All-ages shows.
☎ 310-276-2222 🖳 www .theroxyonsunset.com
✉ 9009 W Sunset Blvd, West Hollywood $ $8-16 (2-drink min) ☽ schedule varies 🚍 MTA 2

Spaceland (5, J6)
At the epicenter of Silver Lake's underground scene, local alternative-rock, indie, skate-punk and surf bands take the stage at Spaceland, all hoping to make it big. Show up early, and look for the neon 'Dreams' sign above the door.
☎ 323-661-4380
🖳 www.clubspaceland.com
✉ 1717 Silver Lake Blvd, Silver Lake $ $3-20, free Mon ☽ shows nightly
🚍 MTA 201

Troubadour (5, C4)
With 'music served fresh since 1957,' the Troubadour draws a mixed, attitude-free crowd of scenesters and jailbait. The musical lineup is fresh, ranging from East Coast acoustic to Japanese punk. Need better views? Head upstairs to the balcony.
☎ 310-276-6168 🖳 www .troubadour.com ✉ 9081 Santa Monica Blvd, West Holly-wood $ $5-20 ☽ shows almost nightly 🚍 MTA 4

Whisky a Go Go (5, C3)
After more than 40 years on the hard-rockin' circuit, this not-quite-so-hip place can still paint the town red. Acts include local artists and LA-born stars. It'll always be the place that launched Jim Morrison and go-go dancing back in the '60s.
☎ 310-652-4202
🖳 www.whiskyagogo.com
✉ 8901 W Sunset Blvd, West Hollywood $ $10-15
☽ shows almost nightly
🚍 MTA 2

GAY & LESBIAN LA

In LA, sexual ambiguity is par for the course. Many of these venues won't look askance at the stray straight patron, while more mainstream bars (p58) and dance clubs (p59) also welcome queer folk.

Abbey (5, C4)
With a svelte coffeehouse vibe, four full bars attract a mixed, low-key crowd to their leafy patios. Patrons unwind after work and sip raspberry martinis under the stars. Bitchy, beautiful boys can be found lounging next door at Here (5, C4).
☎ 310-289-8410 ✉ 692 N Robertson Blvd, West Hollywood ☽ 8pm-2am 🚍 MTA 220 ♿

Akbar (5, H6)
Escape the WeHo scene to this dark, exotic spot in Silver Lake, where a sexually diverse crowd is welcomed, but the mainstays are laid-back hipster boys comparing tattoos around the punk, rockabilly and alt-everything jukebox.
☎ 323-665-6810 ✉ 4356 W Sunset Blvd, Silver Lake ☽ 7pm-2am 🚍 MTA 2

A perfect match at Abbey

Celebration Theatre (5, F3)
It only has 64 seats, but ranks among the nation's leading producers of gay and lesbian plays, winning many awards and staging world premieres. Queer and multicultural perspectives are highlighted.
☎ 323-957-1884 🖳 www.celebrationtheatre.com ✉ 7051 Santa Monica Blvd, Hollywood 🚍 MTA 304 ♿

Factory/Ultra Suede (5, C4)
A couple of million bucks have revamped this sleek twin disco set that claims the biggest dance floors in WeHo. Follow the high-energy crowd to Friday's Girl Bar or men's Action on Saturday nights, with Reflex after-hours.
☎ 310-659-4551 🖳 www.factorynightclub.com

✉ 652 N La Peer Dr, West Hollywood 💲 cover varies ☽ Wed, Fri & Sat 🚍 MTA 4

Hamburger Mary's (5, D3)
This flamboyant franchise eatery puts everyone in a gay mood with drinks specials, weekend brunches and special events. You won't even mind the bill: it's served in a stylish stiletto. Also in Long Beach (3, D4).
☎ 323-654-3800 🖳 www.hamburgermarysweho.com ✉ 8288 Santa Monica Blvd, West Hollywood ☽ 11am-midnight Mon-Thu, 11am-1am Fri & Sat, 10am-midnight Sun 🚍 MTA 4 ♿

Rage (5, C3)
It's the WeHo fave, and all-round hot spot. Expect some attitude at this multistory dance club, where there's plenty of buzz from the eye candy, including chiseled bartenders. Themes vary nightly, from Latin to leather.
☎ 310-652-7055 🖳 www.ragewesthollywood.com ✉ 8911 Santa Monica Blvd, West Hollywood 💲 cover varies ☽ until 2am nightly 🚍 MTA 304

WEHO 90069
In West Hollywood (www.westhollywood.com), Santa Monica Blvd is the G-spot for gay and lesbian nightlife. A more low-key vibe pervades Silver Lake, where bars are far more mixed. The beach towns, historically havens of queerness, have the most relaxed, neighborly scenes, especially in Santa Monica, Venice and Long Beach. LA Pride (p57) and Sunset Junction Street Fair (p57) are big summer parties.

CINEMAS

Discount matinees are before 6pm on weekdays, or the first daily screening on weekends. For listings, check newspapers (p89) or **Moviefone** (☎ 777-3456; www .moviefone.com). Avoid long lines and sell-out shows by buying tickets in advance for a small surcharge.

ArcLight Cinemas (5, G2)
At the historic Cinerama Dome, ArcLight's high-tech multiplex is a romp through 1960s-style decor. New releases, director's cuts and classic revivals are shown in the main hall of the dome. There's a full bar and souvenir shop in the lobby.
☎ 323-464-4226
🖳 www.arclightcinemas.com
✉ 6360 W Sunset Blvd, Hollywood $ $14/10
🚇 MTA 2 P 4hr validated $1
&♿ ♦

Egyptian Theatre (5, B1)
In the same year King Tut's tomb was discovered, this mock-Egyptian temple screened its first all-star Hollywood premiere. Stop by on weekends for the documentary *Forever Hollywood* ($7/5). Run by the nonprofit American Cinematheque, an adventurous art-house calendar screens independent, avant-garde and foreign films, including 'meet the director' events. Also at Santa Monica's Aero Theatre (4, B1).
☎ 323-466-3456
🖳 americancinematheque .com ✉ 6712 Hollywood Blvd, Hollywood $ $9/7
🚇 Hollywood/Highland
&♿ ♦

El Capitan Theatre (5, B1)
Its ornate Spanish colonial facade and East Indian–inspired interior premiered Orson Welles' *Citizen Kane*. Now first-run and classic Disney films get the royal treatment with glittering curtains, often swept back for live-show extravaganzas. Assisted-listening devices are available.
☎ 800-347-6396
🖳 http://disney.go.com
✉ 6838 Hollywood Blvd, Hollywood $ from $12/9
🚇 Hollywood/Highland
& advanced seating

Grauman's Chinese Theatre (5, A1)
Mill around the forecourt of impresario Sid Grauman's famous Hollywood movie palace, dating from 1927. The facade is a fantasy of imperial Chinese architecture. Inside, the theaters show first-run mainstream releases.
☎ 323-464-8111
🖳 www.manntheatres.com
✉ 6801 Hollywood Blvd, Hollywood $ $11/8
🚇 Hollywood/Highland
&♿ ♦

Nuart Theatre
In the shadow of the San Diego Fwy, Nuart screens movies no one else will show. In-person appearances by independent filmmakers are as popular as *The Rocky Horror Picture Show* that screens every Saturday at midnight.
☎ 310-281-8223
✉ 11272 Santa Monica Blvd, west of I-405, West LA
$ $9.50/7
🚇 MTA 304, BBB 1 &♿

The Bridge: Cinema de Lux (3, C3)
Mainstream movies and IMAX films screen at this space-age cineplex at the edge of town. Sit 'Center Stage' for preshow games, prizes and skits, or in the Director's Hall, which features all-reserved leather armchairs.
☎ 310-568-3375 🖳 www .thebridgecinema.com
✉ Promenade at Howard Hughes Center, 6081 Center Dr, West LA $ $12/8
🚗 off I-405 exit Howard Hughes Pkwy P 4hr validated free &♿ ♦

The pharaohs would be proud, Egyptian Theatre

PERFORMING ARTS

Free outdoor summer performances happen at downtown LA's California Plaza (p19) and other public places year-round, including museums (p20) and the **UCLA campus** (3, B2; ☎ 310-825-2101; www.tickets.ucla.edu) in West LA.

The Actors' Gang (3, C3)
Founded in 1981 by Tim Robbins and other renegade UCLA acting school grads, this stand-out theater stages daring and amusing interpretations of classics, as well as bold new ensemble workshop works.
☎ 323-838-4264
🖳 www.theactorsgang.com
✉ 9070 Venice Blvd, Culver City $ $15-50 ☾ Sep-Jul
🚌 MTA 33, 333 ♿

EvidEnce Room (3, C2)
At the cutting edge of LA's sub-100-seat theater scene, this off-the-beaten-path space is a year-round festival of risk-taking theater run by a co-op of artists and actors. No subject is off-limits, not even Hollywood.
☎ 213-381-7118
🖳 www.evidenceroom.com
✉ 2220 Beverly Blvd, west of N Alvarado St, Koreatown
$ $15-20 🚌 MTA 14 ♿

Ford Amphitheatre (5, G1)
In the shadow of the Hollywood Bowl, at this small outdoor venue no seat is more than 100ft from the stage. It presents an astonishingly far-ranging program of chamber music, contemporary dance and theater, and colorful music from around the world.
☎ 323-461-3673 🖳 www.fordamphitheatre.org
✉ 2580 Cahuenga Blvd E, Hollywood Hills $ $5-40
☾ May-Oct ☉ Universal City, then free shuttle bus
🅿 $1-10 ♿ ♿

Geffen Playhouse (3, B2)
An entrance overgrown with ivy beckons you inside to where a host of stars, such as Annette Bening and Jason Alexander,

have performed challenging and classic works by pivotal American playwrights.
☎ 310-208-5454 🖳 www.geffenplayhouse.com
✉ 10886 Le Conte Ave, north of Wilshire Ave, Westwood
$ $40-95 🚌 MTA 2, 761, BBB 1, 2, 3, 8 ♿ ♿

Highways Performance Space & Gallery (4, B2)
Provoking, often shocking performance art is what emerging artists cook up here. The 'curators' put together cabaret, multimedia shows and unusual festivals, but multicultural contemporary dance recitals are the best.
☎ 310-315-1459 🖳 www.highwaysperformance.org
✉ 1651 18th St, Santa Monica $ $10-25
🚌 BBB 1, 10 ♿

Hollywood Bowl (5, F1)
A natural amphitheater in Daisy Dell canyon, the beloved Bowl has staged symphonies under the stars to Monty Python skits to the debut of a folksinger named Bob Dylan. Now the summer

'Do you think we're a little early, honey?' Hollywood Bowl

Mickey's ears would be in raptures at the Walt Disney Concert Hall

home of the Los Angeles Philharmonic (see below), it also hosts big-name rock, jazz and blues touring acts. Many concert-goers show up early to picnic in the parklike grounds (alcohol allowed).

☎ 323-850-2000
🖳 www.hollywoodbowl.com
✉ 2301 N Highland Ave, Hollywood $ tickets from $1
🕲 late Jun–mid-Sep
🚍 shuttle from Hollywood & Highland (p39) $3 ♿ 🚻

LA Philharmonic

Led by Esa-Pekka Salonen, the world-class LA Phil plays at Walt Disney Concert Hall (p23). Their season runs from October to June, while tickets for summer pops concerts at the Hollywood Bowl (see opposite) sell out just as quickly.

☎ 323-850-2000
🖳 www.laphil.com
$ $35-120, student/senior rush $10 ♿

Music Center of LA County (7, B4)

At this linchpin of the downtown performing arts scene, splashy musicals play to capacity at the Ahmanson Theatre, while the more intimate Mark Taper Forum premieres high-caliber plays. With Plácido Domingo at the helm, the LA Opera has fine-tuned its repertory of classics by master composers, with performances at Dorothy Chandler Pavilion.

☎ theater 213-628-2772, dance 213-972-0711, opera 213-972-8001
🖳 www.musiccenter.org
✉ 135 N Grand Ave, downtown LA
$ ticket prices vary
🚇 Civic Center P $8 ♿

REDCAT (7, B4)

The Roy and Edna Disney/CalArts Theater has emerged as the city's premier venue for avant-garde theater, performance art, dance, readings, film and video. The large gallery showcases experimental talent. The lounge was designed by Frank Gehry.

☎ 213-237-2800
🖳 www.redcat.org
✉ 631 W 2nd St, downtown LA $ $10-45
🚍 DASH A, DD, F ♿

Will Geer Theatricum Botanicum (3, A2)

This fairy-tale natural outdoor amphitheater, founded by TV's Grandpa Walton, was a refuge for actors blacklisted during the McCarthy era. Its summer repertory season performs Shakespeare to Arthur Miller.

☎ 310-455-3723
🖳 www.theatricum.com
✉ 1419 N Topanga Canyon Blvd, Topanga $ $8-25
🕲 Jun-Oct ♿ 🚻

SPORTS

For premier seats or tickets to sold-out events, illegal scalpers circle the entrances to major sports venues. Expect to pay a hefty premium for their services. If the game has already started, you might be able to strike a better deal, though.

The **Los Angeles Dodgers** (☎ 866-363-4377; www.dodgers.com) play major-league baseball between April and September at Elysium Park's Dodger Stadium. Cheap tickets are usually available at the box office on game day. The **Los Angeles Angels of Anaheim** (☎ 714-940-2000; www .angelsbaseball.com) play at Angel Stadium out in Orange County.

Led by former Chicago Bulls head coach Phil Jackson, the **Los Angeles Lakers** (www.nba.com/lakers) are the rivals of the other men's National Basketball Association (NBA) team, the **LA Clippers** (www.nba.com/clippers). The awesome **LA Sparks** (www.wnba.com/sparks) of the women's NBA are led by superstar Lisa Leslie, a gold medal–winning Olympian. All basketball teams play at the Staples Center. The WNBA season (July to August) follows the regular men's NBA season (October to April). Lakers tickets (up to $275) are hardest to come by. You can also catch great hoops action with the **UCLA Bruins** (☎ 310-825-2101; www.uclabruins.com) at Pauley Pavilion.

The city has lost its professional National Football League (NFL) teams, but from February to June the **LA Avengers** (☎ 213-742-7340; www.laavengers.com) play fast-paced, high-scoring arena football at the Staples Center. There's a serious cross-town rivalry between two college football teams, the **USC Trojans** (☎ 213-740-2311; www.usctrojans.com), whose home is the LA Coliseum, and the UCLA Bruins. The regular season (September to November) is followed by the Pac-10 playoffs leading up to Pasadena's Rose Bowl game (below).

Although the glory days of Wayne Gretzky and the 1993 Stanley Cup Finals are long gone, the **LA Kings** (☎ 213-742-7340; www.lakings .com) professional ice-hockey team plays from September to April at the Staples Center.

SPORTING VENUES

Angel Stadium (3, F4; ☎ 714-940-2000; 2000 E Gene Autry Way, off I-5 exit Katella Ave, Anaheim)

Dodger Stadium (7, C2; ☎ 323-224-1448; 1000 Elysian Park Ave, downtown LA; bus MTA 2)

LA Coliseum (3, C3; ☎ 213-741-1338; www.lacoliseum.com; 3911 S Figueroa St, Exposition Park; minibus DASH F)

Pauley Pavilion (3, B2; ☎ 310-825-2946; www.uclabruins.com; 555 Westwood Plaza, north of Wilshire Blvd, Westwood; bus MTA 2, BBB 1, 2, 3, 8, 12)

Rose Bowl Stadium (1, A1; ☎ 626-577-3100; www.rosebowlstadium.com; 1001 Rose Bowl Dr, Pasadena)

Santa Anita Racetrack (Horse racing; p26)

Staples Center (7, A5; ☎ 213-742-7340; www.staplescenter.com; 1111 S Figueroa St, downtown LA; Metro Rail Pico; minibus DASH DD, F)

Sleeping

Where you choose to stay dictates how much you'll pay. For luxury, book into hotels in Beverly Hills, Bel Air or the Sunset Strip. Beach towns are great for soaking up the SoCal vibe, with accommodations varying from overpriced motels to pinnacle resorts. Downtown LA has good-value hotels, but most people won't feel comfortable walking around there after dark. Hollywood can be a crapshoot, with seedy motels and shining-star hotels standing side-by-side. Mid-City motels are better midrange choices.

It's all too easy to spend over $200 on a room that's nothing special. Standard rooms have cable TV, telephone and private bathroom. Midrange accommodations may offer continental breakfast, a swimming pool and free parking. Top-end hotels cater to Industry types with in-room entertainment systems, high-speed Internet access, 24-hour business centers and fitness gyms. Luxury boutique and resort hotels have better perks, like spas and gourmet room service. Many lodgings in California are exclusively nonsmoking; all have at least one disability-accessible room or suite.

Always ask about guest parking, which may cost up to $25 per day. In the following reviews, if the P icon appears without a dollar amount, on-site parking is free. Rooms with ocean views cost extra, but may not live up to your expectations. On weekends, beach properties push up their rates, but hotels catering to business travelers

Hollywood Roosevelt Hotel (p72)

offer discount deals. Prices skyrocket in summer (sometimes by over 50%) and on major holidays (p88).

Peak-season travel (usually summer) is more expensive. Discounts are available for American Automobile Association (AAA) members, senior citizens, military personnel and business travelers. Better yet, take advantage of Internet-only promotional deals by booking online, either through the hotel's own website or via travel discounters like www.orbitz.com, www.travelocity.com or www.priceline.com.

DELUXE

Look for **Shade** (3, B4; ☎ 310-546-4995, 866-987-4233; www.shadehotel.com; 1221 N Valley Dr, Manhattan Beach), a chic hotel and spa, opening soon.

Beverly Hills Hotel (5, A4) Countless Hollywood legends have cavorted inside the tropical garden bungalows of the 'Pink Palace' (p13). Starlets languish by the pool where big deals are still cut. Guests take advantage of finely honed service, complimentary limousine rides to area restaurants and a Wimbledon-champion tennis coach, Alex Olmedo.
☎ 310-276-2251, 800-283-8885 🖥 www.beverlyhillshotel.com ✉ 9641 Sunset Blvd, Beverly Hills 🚌 MTA 2 Ⓟ $28 ♿ ✕ Polo Lounge 🖿

Chateau Marmont (5, D2) Its French-flavored indulgence may look dated, but this 1920s faux-chateau, turned inward like a fortress, still attracts A-list stars with its legendary discretion. Greta Garbo swam in the pool, Natalie Wood cavorted on the lawn with James Dean, and Jim Morrison swung from a drainpipe. Garden cottages are the most romantic.
☎ 323-656-1010, 800-242-8328 🖥 www.chateaumarmont.com ✉ 8221 W Sunset Blvd, West Hollywood 🚌 MTA 2 Ⓟ $25 🖿

Disney's Grand Californian (3, E4) Timber beams tower inside this homage to the Arts-&-Crafts movement, the top choice for lodging at Disneyland. Cushy rooms have triple-sheeted beds, down pillows and custom furnishings. Outside there's a redwood water slide into a swimming pool. Parents can enjoy a night out alone while kids join the supervised in-hotel activities (surcharge applies).
☎ 714-635-2300, reservations 714-956-6425 🖥 www.disneyland.com ✉ 1600 S Disneyland Dr, Anaheim 🚌 p8 Ⓟ ♿ ✕ Napa Rose 🚼 🖿

Shutters on the Beach (4, A3) A cosmopolitan seaside resort, Shutters brags of being the only LA hotel set right on the beach. Of course, most rooms are further back in the complex and don't have views, but they do have flowering trellises, Jacuzzis and flat-screen TVs. Original objets d'art and lithographs by David Hockney and Roy Lichtenstein add atmosphere. ONE Spa (p28) is justly celebrated.
☎ 310-458-0030, 800-334-9000 🖥 www.shuttersonthebeach.com ✉ 1 Pico Blvd, Santa Monica 🚌 BBB 1, 7 Ⓟ $26 ♿ ✕ One Pico 🚼 🖿

TOP END

Avalon Hotel (5, B6) This deliciously ice-blue hotel mixes 21st-century cool with Mid-Century Modern furnishings, harking back to when Marilyn Monroe lived here. In-room spa treatments, high-speed Internet and beautiful people lounging in cabanas by the hourglass-shaped pool are all perks.
☎ 310-277-5221, 800-670-6183 🖥 www.avalonbeverlyhills.com ✉ 9400 W Olympic Blvd, Beverly Hills 🚌 MTA 28, BBB 5 Ⓟ $24 ♿ ✕ blue on blue 🖿

Mum's the word at Chateau Marmont

Beach House at Hermosa Beach (3, C4)

Whatever you've heard about California's laid-back lifestyle, this epitomizes it. Fall asleep to the sound of the surf in large, lofty suites with full or partial ocean views, private balconies, micro-kitchens and wood-burning fireplaces.

☎ 310-374-3001, 888-895-4559 🖥 www.beach-house .com ✉ 1300 The Strand at 14th St, Hermosa Beach 🚊 MTA 439 Ⓟ $20 ♿ 👶

Dockside Boat and Bed (3, D5)

A sense of romance and salt sea spray splash this floating hostelry. Let the waves rock you to dreamland inside your private yacht, or perhaps a 50ft-replica Chinese junk, moored within view of the RMS *Queen Mary*.

☎ 562-436-3111, 800-436-2574 🖥 www.boatandbed .com ✉ Dock 5, Rainbow Harbor, 316 E Shoreline Dr, Long Beach ◉ Transit Mall, then Long Beach Transit bus Pine Ave Link Ⓟ $12 👶

Georgian Hotel (4, A2)

A favorite hideaway of Clark Gable and Carole Lombard, this historic art-deco hotel near Santa Monica Pier has character. Take breakfast on the veranda or in the former speakeasy where gangster

'A boudoir, for moi?' Maison 140.

Bugsy Siegel imbibed. Renovated rooms have Nintendo systems and wi-fi.

☎ 310-395-9945, 800-538-8147 🖥 www.georgianhotel .com ✉ 1415 Ocean Ave, Santa Monica 🚊 BBB 1, 7 Ⓟ $21 ♿ 👶

Maison 140 (5, A5)

Inside the former villa of silent-movie siren Lillian Gish, a Parisian boudoir atmosphere is where French kiss meets Far East fantasy. B&B boutique rooms are smallish, but enjoy high-speed Internet and a full-service concierge. The intimate downstairs cocktail lounge fairly hums after dark.

☎ 310-281-4000, 800-670-6182 🖥 www.maison140 .com ✉ 140 S Lasky Dr, Beverly Hills 🚊 MTA 720 Ⓟ $18 ♿ 🍴 at Avalon Hotel (opposite)

Renaissance Hollywood (5, B1)

If you're imagining a poolside view of the Hollywood sign, this deluxe chain hotel with spacious, amenity-laden rooms next to Hollywood & Highland (p39) will fit the bill. The multilingual staff ensure trouble-free stays.

☎ 323-856-1200, 888-236-2427 🖥 www.renaissance hollywood.com ✉ 1755 N Highland Ave, Hollywood ◉ Hollywood/Highland Ⓟ $10-15 ♿ 🍴 Vert (p48) 👶 🍸

Viceroy (4, A3)

A bland exterior belies the fact that Viceroy brings a touch of Hollywood glamour to the sea. This urban outpost sports a campy British colonial theme and a chic color palette. The bar Cameo (p59) draws socialites from across town, as do in-room and poolside spa services by Fred Segal (p40).

☎ 310-260-7500, 800-670-6185 🖥 www.viceroysanta monica.com ✉ 1819 Ocean Ave, Santa Monica 🚊 Tide Shuttle, BBB 1, 7 Ⓟ $20 ♿ 🍴 Whist 🍸

FOR FAMILIES

Although many motels and hotels advertise 'kids stay free,' you will have to pay extra for a baby cot or a 'roll-away' (portable bed). If you've got tots in tow, look for the child-friendly icon 👶 following reviews in this chapter for your best bets. Many babysitters (p30) are available to come straight to your hotel room.

MIDRANGE

Ambrose (4, B2)
This blissful boutique hotel
blends Arts-&-Crafts and
Asian aesthetics and boasts
all-concierge staff. Lounge
in the tranquil garden with a
koi pond. Some rooms have
balconies with teak furniture.
Rates include a healthy
breakfast.
☎ 310-315-1555, 877-262-
7673 ▯ www.ambrosehotel
.com ✉ 1255 20th St,
Santa Monica ➠ BBB 2, 11
Ⓟ ♿ 🚹

**Best Western Sunset
Plaza Hotel** (5, D2)
This chain hotel puts you right
into the Sunset Strip party
scene, paired with reasonable
prices. It even has suites with
kitchens. Rates include lots of
free stuff, too, like breakfast
and local calls. High-speed
Internet available.
☎ 323-654-0750, 800-421-
3652 ▯ www.bestwestern
.com ✉ 8400 W Sunset Blvd,
West Hollywood ➠ MTA 2
Ⓟ $10 ♿ 🚹 🐾

**Cal Mar Hotel
Suites** (4, A1)
Active families who need
room to move love these

apartment-sized suites with
full kitchens and extra sofa
beds. It's a quick stroll to
the beach. A small pool and
nearby fitness gym make
up for the generic decor and
noise.
☎ 310-395-5555, 800-776-
6007 ▯ www.calmarhotel
.com ✉ 220 California Ave,
Santa Monica ➠ BBB 2, 4
Ⓟ ♿ 🚹 🐾

Farmer's Daughter (5, E5)
After an extreme makeover,
this hotel has a sleek new
'urban cowboy' look that
is an amazing alchemy of
styles. Denim bedspreads
and rocking chairs team up
with artworks, shiny plank
floors and wi-fi. Staff are
ultra-helpful.
☎ 323-937-3930, 800-334-
1658 ▯ www.farmers
daughterhotel.com ✉ 115
S Fairfax Ave, Hollywood
➠ MTA 217 Ⓟ $10
♿ ✕ Original Farmers
Market (p50) 🚹 🐾

Figueroa Hotel (7, A5)
This little tourist hotel has
been going strong since
1905. Its charming colonial
Mexican-style lobby has
colorful tiles, murals and
wrought-iron fixtures.

High-ceilinged rooms have a
dash of color, while suites are
Moroccan-themed.
☎ 213-627-8971, 800-421-
9092 ▯ www.figueroahotel
.com ✉ 939 S Figueroa St,
downtown LA ➠ DASH DD, F
Ⓟ $8 ✕ Cafe & Nomad
♿ 🐾

**Hollywood Roosevelt
Hotel** (5, A1)
Spanish Colonial architecture
and delicious gossip rendez-
vous at this newly reinvented
hotel, a Hollywood fixture
since 1927. Only the poolside
cabana rooms still wear that
retro look. Service is spotty,
and it's noisy here –what
you're paying for is the A-list
scene.
☎ 323-466-7000, 800-950-
7667 ▯ www.hollywood
roosevelt.com ✉ 7000
Hollywood Blvd, Hollywood
Ⓜ Hollywood/Highland
Ⓟ $23 ♿
✕ Dakota (p48) 🐾

Magic Castle Hotel (5, F2)
Renovated rooms feature
trendy blond-wood furniture;
families will love the full-
kitchen suites. Start your
day with fresh pastries and
gourmet coffee by the pool.
Guests can pay to visit the
adjacent Magic Castle, a
fabled private magic club in a
Victorian mansion.
☎ 323-851-0800, 800-741-
4915 ▯ www.magic
castlehotel.com ✉ 7025
Franklin Ave, Hollywood
Ⓜ Hollywood/Highland
Ⓟ $8 ♿ 🚹 🐾

Omni Hotel (7, B4)
Modern and efficient, this
business hotel at California
Plaza puts you within steps
of the MOCA, the Walt Disney

Cast a holiday spell at Magic Castle Hotel

Yeah, best to do them in that order

Concert Hall and other downtown cultural hubs. Welcome assets include a rooftop pool, oversized rooms and high-speed Internet.
☎ 213-617-3300, 888-444-6664 ⬚ www.omnihotels.com ✉ 251 S Olive St, downtown LA
🚇 DASH A, B, DD 🅿 $24 ♿ 🍴 Noé (p47) ♿ 🛆

Orlando (5, D5)
A unique boutique hotel that makes it worth staying near the Beverly Center (p39), the Orlando is a soothing, earth-toned hideaway amid the 3rd St 'gourmet ghetto.' Keep fit with a gym and outdoor heated saltwater pool. In-room high-speed Internet available.
☎ 323-658-6600, 800-624-6835 ⬚ www.theorlando.com ✉ 8384 W 3rd St, Mid-City 🚇 MTA 16 🅿 $19 ♿ 🍴 La Terza 🛆

The Standard (7, B4)
This downtown hotel – in the redesigned Superior Oil headquarters – goes after the same young, hip and shag-happy crowd as its older Sunset Strip sibling (5, D3). Rooms have a platform bed, peek-through shower and little else in the way of furniture, but smoking is allowed in some. Rooftop Bar (p59) is an intense pick-up scene.
☎ 213-892-8080 ⬚ www.standardhotel.com ✉ 550 S Flower St, downtown LA 🚇 7th St/Metro Center 🅿 $25 ♿ 🍴 Restaurant (p50) 🛆

Venice Beach House (4, A5)
Carpeted by flowers a block from the beach, this Arts-&-Crafts home (built in 1911 and listed on the National Register of Historic Places) is a welcoming old-California B&B with nine cozy rooms

and suites, some with shared bathrooms.
☎ 310-823-1966 ⬚ www.venicebeachhouse.com ✉ 15 30th Ave, Venice 🚇 MTA 108 🅿 $10 ♿

BUDGET

Banana Bungalow Hollywood @ the Orbit
(5, E4)
This convivial hostel puts the 'mod' in modern. Its location near LA's epicenter of youthful hipness makes it a standout. Some of the good-sized private rooms even have balconies. High-speed Internet, plus free luggage storage and LAX shuttle pick-up, is available.
☎ 323-655-1510, 800-446-7835 ⬚ www.bananabungalow.com ✉ 7950 Melrose Ave, West Hollywood 🚇 MTA 10, 11, DASH Fairfax 🅿

Beverly Laurel Motor Hotel (5, D4)
An artsy retro motor lodge if ever there was one (and it's pet-friendly, too). Rooms with turquoise doors wrap around a heated courtyard pool. Kitchenettes cost just $15 extra, but the real draw is the downstairs coffee shop, Swingers (p50).
☎ 323-651-2441; fax 323-651-5225 ✉ 8018 Beverly Blvd, Mid-City 🚇 MTA 14 🅿 ♿ 🍴 Swingers ♿ 🛆

Culver Hotel (3, C3)
Once owned by John Wayne, this tall hotel in out-of-the-way downtown Culver City is a stone's throw from the movie studio where *The Wizard of Oz* was filmed. Plain rooms aren't fancy, but

are furnished with antiques at least.

☎ 310-838-7963, 888-328-5837 🖳 www.culverhotel .com ✉ 9400 Culver Blvd, at Washington Blvd, Culver City 🚌 MTA 220 ♿ ✖ Scarlet 🚹

Hollywood Celebrity Hotel (5, A1)

Hidden behind Hollywood & Highland (p39), the art-deco lobby is a promising overture, but it contrasts with the rooms that are a bit long in the tooth. Still, most are spacious, some have high-speed Internet and those with full kitchens are a deal.

Forget about parking – it's a headache.

☎ 323-850-6464, 800-222-7017 🖳 www.hotelcelebrity .com ✉ 1775 Orchid Ave, Hollywood ⊖ Hollywood & Highland 🅿 🚹

Sea Shore Motel (4, A3)

This little motel is one of a dying breed: a clean, budget-priced place mere steps from the beach, bars, boutiques and restaurants. The redone rooms have refrigerators, cable TV and window air-con units. Expect some street noise.

☎ 310-392-2787 🖳 www.seashoremotel.com

✉ 2637 Main St, Santa Monica 🚌 Tide Shuttle, BBB 1, 10 🅿 ♿ 🚹

Villa Brasil Motel (3, B3)

With a cheery colorful facade, this spruced-up little motel sits on otherwise drab Washington Blvd, not too far from Sony Pictures Studios (p27). The tropical flair continues in the basic rooms, which come with ceiling fans. Kitchenettes available.

☎ 310-636-0141 🖳 www .villabrasilmotel.com ✉ 11740 Washington Blvd, west of I-405, Culver City 🅿 ♿ 🚹

GAY & LESBIAN ACCOMMODATION

Any hotel in West Hollywood (WeHo) can be safely assumed to be gay-friendly. A block away from the velocity of the Sunset Strip, the eccentric **Secret Garden B&B** (5, D2; ☎ 323-656-3888, 877-732-4736; www.secretgardenbnb.com; 8039 Selma Ave, West Hollywood) has a romantic Rapunzel tower tucked away in a dreamy garden. Worth a trip down to Long Beach, the stately Victorian **Turret House** (3, D4; ☎ 562-624-1991, 888-488-7738; www.turrethouse.com; 556 Chestnut Ave at 6th St, Long Beach) is also gay-owned – *and* pet-friendly. For more options, click to www.purpleroofs.com.

She doesn't look like a damsel in distress – Turret House

About Los Angeles

HISTORY
City of Angels
The earliest residents of the Los Angeles Basin were coastal Chumash and Tongva (Gabrieleño) tribes of Native Americans. Both peoples were animistic, with warfare rare and horses unknown before the arrival of Spanish colonists, starting in 1542 with Juan Cabrillo's explorations along the Southern California coast.

It's a Mex fest! Cinco de Mayo festival.

In 1769 Father Junípero Serra and Spanish soldier and colonial governor Don Gasper de Portolà led an expedition into Alta (Upper) California, from San Diego north to Monterey. Of the 21 missions eventually established along El Camino Real (The Royal Highway), Mission San Gabriel Archangel (3, D2) and Mission San Fernando Rey de España (3, B1) stand in valleys near LA.

For Native Americans, the mission era was a bitter deal. They traded hard labor for promises of salvation – and European diseases, such as smallpox and syphilis. Pueblo towns of Mexican settlers encroached on traditional tribal lands. Spanish military presidios designed to protect the missions were filled with rowdy soldiers who were often abusive and rarely paid.

In 1781 a small band of *pobladores*, or *mestizo* (mixed-blood) settlers, established a new pueblo on the banks of a stream shaded by cottonwood. They named it El Pueblo de Nuestra Señora la Reina de los Angeles del Río Porciúncula, in honor of a saint whose feast day had just passed. Although it lacked a navigable river or reliable supply route, the pueblo soon thrived on bountiful orange and olive groves, vineyards and grazing lands.

WATER FOR A THIRSTY GIANT
LA's growth from a semi-arid desert into a sprawling metropolis is inextricably linked to water, or the lack thereof.

In 1913 William Mulholland, the city's most infamous waterworks superintendent, opened the controversial LA aqueduct, which diverted (some say 'stole') water from the farms of the Owens Valley over 220 miles away.

Mulholland is memorialized by Roman Polanski's fictional noir film *Chinatown*, starring Jack Nicholson and Faye Dunaway, and the celebrated Mulholland Drive, which starts west of the Hollywood Reservoir and once flowed unbroken all the way to the Pacific Ocean.

Home on the Rancho

After 1821, many citizens of newly independent Mexico looked to California to satisfy their thirst for private land. By the mid-1830s, the mission system had crumbled and Mexican governors were doling out hundreds of free land grants. 'Rancheros,' as the new landowners were called, quickly became the social, cultural and political heart of California. After the USA annexed Texas in 1845, Mexico cut diplomatic relations and ordered foreigners out of California. The 1848 Treaty of Guadalupe Hidalgo ended the Mexican-American War and made California part of the USA. It was admitted as the 31st state of the Union, thanks to the gold-rush fever of American settlers.

Gold Rush to the Silver Screen

In 1850, the same year as the city was incorporated, LA was an unruly town of dirt streets with hard-drinking saloons, brothels and gambling dens. After the gold rush peaked, the state was thrust into depression. Some citizens turned to highway robbery, first of Wells Fargo stagecoaches and later of the transcontinental railroad in the 1870s. The railroad's completion also drove immigration and the expansion of the orange-growing industry in California.

At the turn of the 20th century, oil production in the Los Angeles Basin brought a new rush of people out West. The city's population soared to almost one million by 1920. Noting the ideal test-flight weather, the Loughead brothers and Glenn Martin established aircraft-manufacturing plants that helped the city lift out of the Great Depression and to grow throughout WWII and the Cold War. The railway and defense industries continued to draw new immigrants, especially African Americans.

But more than anything else, the film industry came to symbolize Los Angeles. Motion-picture producers were drawn to LA as early as 1906 by the sunny SoCal climate. Any type of location could be shot easily – and cheaply – here. Studios were constructed in Culver City and Universal City, but the capital of filmdom was the newly fashionable suburb of Hollywood.

SURF'S UP!

The ancient royal Hawaiian sport of surfing was popularized in Southern California by Hawaiian-Irish surfer George Freeth, who miraculously 'walked on water' at Redondo Beach (3, C4) in 1907. Growing up in Hawaii, Freeth had seen a Polynesian painting showing his mother's ancestors riding the waves, and decided to try his luck. After gargantuan, traditional 16ft-hardwood boards proved too hard to handle, he cut one in half, thus creating the first 'long board.' Freeth eventually became SoCal's first lifeguard, but died in the great influenza epidemic of 1919, making his short, sweet life the original 'endless summer.'

SHAKE, RATTLE & ROLL

Los Angeles straddles one of the world's major earthquakes zones. The great San Andreas Fault comes within 33 miles of downtown, while dozens of minor faults crisscross the metropolis like cracks on an eggshell. The 1994 Northridge earthquake, measuring 6.7 on the Richter scale, had its epicenter in the San Fernando Valley and ended up being the most costly quake in US history – at least, so far. Your chances of being in town when the next Big One hits are only slightly higher, however, than the odds of Godzilla eating Tokyo.

LA Today

Los Angeles has been defined and defied by its multiethnicity. Politicians turned a blind eye to racial tensions for decades, resulting in the 1943 Zoot Suit Riots, the unjust deportation of Japanese Americans to WWII internment camps, and the burning of the Watts neighborhood – first in August 1965 during the civil-rights era and again in 1992 after the acquittal of police officers accused of savagely beating an African American suspect, Rodney King. Heavy flooding, wild brush fires and the 1994 Northridge earthquake made for a difficult passage into the 21st century.

ENVIRONMENT

LA's infamous smog, a yellowish layer of toxic fumes that hangs over the skyline, is a by-product of car and factory emissions. Ozone levels peak during summer, which also brings the greatest number of inversion days, when a layer of warm air traps the noxious fumes. Tough environmental regulations have helped to spur a recent decline in air pollution.

Another LA day on the 'freeway'

The city's rising population contends with an ongoing crisis in natural resources. Aqueducts deliver 85% of LA water from rivers far outside the megalopolis. The state experienced one of its worst-ever droughts in the early 1990s. Deregulation of public utilities led to the energy crisis of 2000–01.

For most Californians, eco-friendly practices – such as recycling, daily water-use reduction, car-pool lanes and alternative energy sources like solar and wind power – have been a part of everyday life since the 1970s.

GOVERNMENT & POLITICS

The city of Los Angeles is governed by a mayor and a council of 15 members, each elected for four-year terms. Currently, the council reflects the diversity that is characteristic of Los Angeles. Mayor Antonio Villaraigosa, an energetic Democratic labor leader elected in 2005, has already made waves by vowing to find new answers to the city's intractable problems of economic disparity, overpopulation, limited natural resources and traffic by focusing on fixing freeways, schools and policing. Relations between the new mayor and celebrity Governor Arnold Schwarzenegger, a Republican, are so far cordial.

Traditionally LA has been predominantly Democrat, while outlying areas such as Orange County and the next-closest major city, San Diego, are Republican. Longtime separatists from LA politics are Santa Monica, Pasadena and Beverly Hills. Although these mini-

LA's sister cities – that's one big family!

cities cooperate with City Hall, they independently manage their own budgets and affairs. Hollywood and the San Fernando Valley were unsuccessful secession candidates in 2002.

DID YOU KNOW?
- Los Angeles averages almost 300 days of sunshine per year
- the city ranks 36th nationally in per-capita crime, behind even some Midwestern cities
- nearly 23 million tourists stay overnight here each year
- entry-level workers are paid $6.75 per hour; Julia Roberts gets $20 million per movie
- the median price of a single-family home in Beverly Hills is $1.25 million
- LA is the only US city to host the summer Olympics twice, in 1932 and 1984

ECONOMY

LA benefited from the strong national economy in the late 1990s, but major economic restructuring – moving away from the traditional aerospace, entertainment and tourism industries, the last of which alone rakes in over $11 billion annually – was primarily responsible for improved balance sheets. Unemployment hovers at around 6%, slightly above the national average.

LA County is the largest manufacturing center in the USA, and has the nation's largest port for international trade. The Industry, as the motion-picture business is known, continues to pay, thanks to insatiable viewer demand, and supports over a quarter of a million jobs. Software development and other high-tech industries also flourish, notably driven by Boeing and DirecTV. LA is a center for new design, be it of cars, fashion or furniture, and also higher education, with over 170 college and university campuses. Service jobs are by far the biggest sector, even without counting illegal immigrants who work off the books.

SOCIETY & CULTURE

LA County has 10 million inhabitants, accounting for over 25% of California's total population, while the city of LA proper has almost four million people. Almost half of all Angelenos are Latino, 30% are Caucasian, 11% African American and 10% Asian; Native Americans and Pacific Islanders together make up less than 1% of the population.

The spice of life – you'll find it in LA

Nearly half of California's Spanish-speaking population resides in LA County. In fact, East Los Angeles boasts the largest concentration of Mexicans outside Mexico. The city also has some of the largest US metro-area populations of Asian immigrants, including Japanese, Koreans, Thais and Cambodians. In traditional Jewish neighborhoods, such as Fairfax Ave, orthodox men and women still shop at kosher delis.

Diversity looks good on paper, but minority groups have often had rough treatment. African American neighborhoods built through segregation have suffered disproportionately from violent crime and a lack of infrastructure. Mexican and Latin American workers still do most of the farm labor and domestic work in the state.

Dos & Don'ts

California is famous for its laissez-faire social standards. As for fashion, anything goes (and a vintage T-shirt and hipster jeans will take you from Beverly Hills to the beach). However, smoking is prohibited in all public

---

CELLULOID NARCISSUS

Although the Hollywood blockbuster has become synonymous with brainless twaddle, Robert Altman's *The Player* (1992) is a smart, sardonic attack on Hollywood, while Steve Martin's slightly dated *LA Story* (1991) is hilariously true-to-life. The classic piece on the perils of stardom is Billy Wilder's *Sunset Boulevard* (1950). More moody meditations on life outside the studio gates include Roman Polanski's *Chinatown* (1974); Ridley Scott's futuristic noir *Blade Runner* (1982); John Singleton's *Boyz N the Hood* (1991); Quentin Tarantino's *Pulp Fiction* (1994); David Lynch's surrealist *Mulholland Drive* (2001); and indie flick *Laurel Canyon* (2002), starring Frances McDormand.

---

places. Do not litter or jaywalk, especially in well-to-do neighborhoods where police may fine you. Recycle wherever possible.

Keep pets on a leash outdoors at all times. When roller-blading, cycling or walking along the beach boardwalks, keep to the side and don't switch lanes. Surfers who drop in on a wave already being surfed risk harassment back on shore.

Road rage is a serious problem. On LA's infamous freeways, cutting other drivers off, speeding and nonstop honking comprise typically rude behavior; drive defensively. Rumors of freeway shootings are not urban legends. Take heart though – they're not the norm.

ARTS

Throughout the 20th century, LA has been a mecca for artistic talent, both native and imported, making it quite the opposite of the cultural black hole many expect.

Film

A powerful worldwide export, the Industry grew out of the humble orchards of Hollywoodland. When the silent-movie era gave way to 'talkies' after 1927's *The Jazz Singer* premiered downtown, Hollywood's glamorous Golden Age had arrived. The city's first TV station started broadcasting in 1931.

Today Hollywood is no longer the focus of the silver screen, although the Industry nets the city a cool $30 billion annually. Most films and TV shows are shot on studio backlots over in Burbank. The high cost of filming in LA has recently sent location scouts up to Canada, nicknamed 'Hollywood North.'

And the Oscar goes to...the guy in the T-shirt

'Hey, have you got that one by, you know, that cool band...?' Amoeba Music (p42)

Literature

During the 1940s, F Scott Fitzgerald, Ernest Hemingway and Tennessee Williams all did stints as Hollywood screenwriters. Novelists and journalists have also found the city fecund. Charles Bukowski, Joan Didion, Hunter S Thomspon and Bret Easton Ellis have all skewered LA in their writings. King of the hard-boiled crime writers was Raymond Chandler, who thinly disguised his hometown of Santa Monica as 'Bay City.' A 1990s renaissance of crime fiction was masterminded by James Ellroy *(LA Confidential)*, Elmore Leonard *(Jackie Brown)* and Walter Mosley *(Devil in a Blue Dress)*.

Music

Exiled European composers who migrated to LA prior to WWII included Igor Stravinsky. Big swing bands toured here during the war. Later bebop played by Charlie Parker and Charlie Mingus made the city hum. The cool West Coast jazz pioneered by Miles Davis evolved in the 1950s, just as doo-wop, rhythm and blues, and soul music grew strong in South Central's nightclubs.

Rock 'n' roll found a revolutionary home here from its natal years. In the 1950s, Richie Valens' 'La Bamba' made a rockified version of a Mexican folk song. Surf music began strumming at the beaches that same decade. In the heady '60s, Jim Morrison and The Doors burst onto the Sunset Strip.

LA today is a hotbed for West Coast rap and hip-hop. What began as a grassroots art form has become one of the city's money-making cultural exports, from baggy jeans to multimillion-dollar movie deals. Eazy-E, Ice Cube and Dr. Dre from the seminal group NWA (Niggaz With Attitude) have all founded their own record labels.

Architecture

LA's architecture is as diverse as its population.

Adobe houses and early colonial buildings adopted the Spanish Mission style. During the late 19th century, California's upper class built grand Victorian mansions. After the turn of the 20th century, the California bungalow evolved, with finely worked Arts & Crafts details and harmonious natural elements.

Art deco and Streamline Moderne took off by the 1920s and into the '30s. Austrian immigrants Richard Neutra and Rudolph Schindler developed the California Modernist style that still influences the postmodern giants of today, Frank Gehry and Richard Meier.

Googie architecture, a futuristic style of roadside vernacular design, became popular in the 1950s and '60s, especially at SoCal bowling alleys and coffee shops.

Streamline Moderne - a beauty all of its own

Theater & Dance

Home to 25% of the nation's professional actors, LA is the second-most influential city in America for theater, behind only New York City. Famous faces play on stage beside talented amateurs, and important playwrights launch their premieres here. Small theaters flourish at the edges of West Hollywood (WeHo) and North Hollywood (NoHo), the West Coast's answer to off- and off-off-Broadway, respectively. Martha Graham, Alvin Ailey and Bella Lewitzky were among LA's pioneers of modern dance.

Visual Arts

The turn of the 20th century saw an influx of landscape painters seeking inspiration from California's natural beauty. During the Depression, abstract expressionist Jackson Pollock painted for the Works Progress Administration (WPA). In 1940 Man Ray brought surrealism and dadaism, while Salvador Dalí designed film sets for Alfred Hitchcock and was employed by Walt Disney. By the 1960s, pop artists like Wayne Thiebaud became obsessed by consumerism, technology and urban travails. The same themes are explored by LA artists today, notably British émigré David Hockney. Judith Baca is an active Chicana muralist.

ARRIVAL & DEPARTURE
Air
About 17 miles southwest of downtown LA, nine-terminal **Los Angeles International Airport** (LAX; 3, B3; ☎ 310-646-5252; www.lawa.org/lax) is close to the coast. Mid-sized LA County airports include Burbank's **Bob Hope Airport** (BUR; 3, C1; ☎ 818-840-8840; www.bobhopeairport .com) and **Long Beach Airport** (LGB; 3, D4; ☎ 562-570-2619).

LOS ANGELES INTERNATIONAL AIRPORT
Information
Airport police (☎ 310-646-7911)
General information (☎ 310-646-5252)
Parking information (☎ 310-646-9070)
Travelers Aid (☎ 310-646-2270)

Foreign currency exchange and ATMs are found in every terminal. The Tom Bradley International Terminal has a **first-aid station** (☎ 310-215-6000; ☼ 10am-10pm) on the departures level, and you can rent cell phones on the lower level. There's an Internet café in Terminal 4. Baggage storage is not available post-9/11.

Airport Access
Free shuttle buses connect LAX's passenger terminals.

Parking spaces in the central area cost $3 for the first hour and $2 per additional hour. Remote lots B and C offer two hours of free parking, long-term rates and free airport shuttles.

All airport transport services depart outside the arrivals level at each terminal. Some shared-ride van shuttles like **Prime Time** (☎ 800-733-8267; www.primetime shuttle.com) and **SuperShuttle** (☎ 800-258-3826; www.supershuttle.com) operate 24 hours between the airports and LA-area hotels for $10 to $20 per person. **Coach USA** (☎ 714-938-8937, 800-828-6699)

offers hourly motor-coach services to Anaheim ($19/16, 45 minutes).

From LAX, take free Shuttle G to Metro Rail's Aviation station. Green Line trains depart frequently for Imperial/Wilmington 15 minutes away, where you can transfer to the Blue Line downtown to 7th St/Metro Center (25 minutes), which connects with the Red Line west to Hollywood or east to Union Station, where you can again transfer to the Gold Line north to Pasadena. The one-way fare is $1.25. From LAX, free Shuttle C goes to the city bus center, from where you can catch buses in any direction, including Big Blue Bus 3 (75¢, 20 to 30 minutes, 5:30am to midnight) to Santa Monica and UCLA.

Car-rental agencies offer free airport pickups and drop-offs. Approximate taxi fares from LAX are: Santa Monica $20 to $25, Beverly Hills $25 to $30, Hollywood $35 to $40 and downtown $40.

Train
The national rail service, **Amtrak** (☎ 800-872-7245; www.amtrak.com), services major US cities. Scenic coastal routes connect LA with San Diego, Santa Barbara and Oakland, but trains are not always punctual. In downtown LA, trains arrive and depart from **Union Station** (7, D4; ☎ 213-683-6729; 800 N Alameda St; ☼ 24hr).

Bus
Reliable **Greyhound** (☎ 800-231-2222; www.greyhound.com) operates extensive, if slow, routes across North America. Its main terminal (7, C6; ☎ 213-629-8401; 1716 E 7th St; ☼ 24hr) is in downtown LA. Other terminals include Hollywood and Anaheim.

Travel Documents
PASSPORT
Your passport must be valid for at least six months from your date of entry. Canadians will be required to carry a passport to enter the USA by late 2006.

VISA

Currently visas aren't required for visits up to 90 days for citizens of the EU, Australia and New Zealand, as long as they present a machine-readable passport upon arrival.

All other travelers need a visa, which can be obtained at most US embassies and consulates overseas; however, it is usually easier to obtain a visa in your home country.

It's important to check with the US Department of State's **Bureau of Consular Affairs** (☎ 202-663-1225; www.travel .state.gov/visa) for the latest information.

RETURN/ONWARD TICKET

A round-trip ticket to any foreign destination, other than US-adjacent islands, is required to enter the country.

Customs & Duty Free

You can import, duty-free: 1L of alcohol, if you're over 21; 200 cigarettes, 50 cigars or 2kg of tobacco, if you're over 18; and gifts totaling $100 ($800 for US citizens). Travelers with more than $10,000 in currency or cash equivalents must declare it upon entry. Importing food is usually prohibited, as are all illegal drugs and any goods made in Cuba or other embargoed countries. For the latest regulations, contact **US Customs & Border Protection** (☎ 202-354-1000; www.cbp.gov).

GETTING AROUND

LA is a notoriously auto-dependent city. You can get around by public transit, but the system is limited and often requires chunks of time. In this book, the nearest metro station (⊕) or bus route (🚌) is noted after each review.

Travel Passes

The **Metropolitan Transit Authority** (MTA; ☎ 800-266-6883, TTY/TDD 800-252-9040; www.mta.net) sells day ($3) and weekly ($14) passes, valid on both MTA buses and Metro Rail trains. They are sold at 850 retail outlets around town and at MTA customer centers, including **Union Station** (7, D4; 🕑 6am-6:30pm Mon-Fri) and **Mid-City** (5, F6; 5301 Wilshire Blvd; 🕑 9am-5pm Mon-Fri).

Metro Rail

Operated by MTA, Metro Rail light-rail trains connect downtown with Hollywood and Universal City (Red Line), Pasadena (Gold Line), LAX (Green Line) and Long Beach (Blue Line). One-way fares are $1.25. Trains run approximately 5am to midnight daily.

Bus

A network of bus routes spans the metropolis, with most operated by MTA. Its base one-way fare is $1.25 (75¢ after 9pm), up to $2.25 for freeway routes; bring exact change. Most routes operate 5am to 2am daily.

Fast, frequent Metro Rapid buses (numbered in the 700s) make limited stops. No 720 travels downtown from Santa Monica via Westwood, Beverly Hills and Mid-City's Miracle Mile along Wilshire Blvd in just 45 to 70 minutes.

DASH MINIBUSES

For quick hops, DASH minibuses (☎ 808-2273, 800-266-6883; www.ladottransit .com) cost just 25¢. Downtown DASH Routes A to F run every five to 20 minutes from 6:30am to 6:30pm weekdays, with limited service on weekends. Of the two-dozen neighborhood DASH routes, the Fairfax, Hollywood, and Hollywood/West Hollywood minibuses are most useful for visitors.

BIG BLUE BUS

Santa Monica's efficient **Big Blue Bus** (☎ 310-451-5444; www.bigbluebus.com) system connects much of the Westside, including Beverly Hills, Westwood/UCLA and Venice. Schedules vary, depending on the route. One-way fares are 75¢, transfers 25¢. Line 10 Freeway Express to downtown LA costs $1.75. Big Blue Bus routes are abbreviated with 'BBB' in reviews in this book. The Tide Shuttle (25¢) departs Santa Monica Place for Venice Beach via Ocean Ave, returning north via Main St, every 15 minutes from noon to 10pm (to midnight Friday and Saturday).

Car & Motorcycle

Most Angelenos never use public transit, thus traffic can be excruciating. Avoid the freeways during rush hours (5am to 9am and 3pm to 7pm), beachfront highways on weekends and the Sunset Strip after dark. For frequent traffic reports, tune to KNX 1070AM or KFWB 980AM.

Major freeways:

I-5	Golden State/Santa Ana Fwy
I-10	Santa Monica/San Bernardino Fwy
I-110	Pasadena/Harbor Fwy
I-405	San Diego Fwy
I-710	Long Beach Fwy
US 101	Hollywood/Ventura Fwy
Hwy 1	Pacific Coast Hwy

On-street parking is tight, but not impossible to find. It is usually metered and/or restricted, so obey posted signs to avoid pricey parking tickets. Private lots and parking garages cost at least $5 per day. Valet parking costs as much as $30. Municipal lots, like in Beverly Hills and near Santa Monica Place, are free for a certain time limit. Gasoline (petrol) is inexpensive by foreign standards, averaging almost $3 per US gallon (78¢ per liter) at press time, though this quoted price is highly subject to change.

RENTAL

Rental starts at $20 per day or $120 per week. Major car-rental companies found at airports and around town include **Alamo** (☎ 800-462-5266; www.alamo.com), **Dollar** (☎ 800-800-4000; www.dollar.com) and **Thrifty** (☎ 800-367-2277; www.thrifty.com). No one rents to drivers under 21. Some may rent to drivers under 25, but will tack on hefty surcharges.

ROAD RULES

Drive on the right side of the road. Turn right at a red light only after stopping, if signs do not prohibit it. Seat belts must be worn (helmets for motorcyclists) and parents must use child-safety seats for under-fours.

Unless otherwise posted, the speed limit is 65mph on freeways and 35mph on city streets. Diamond HOV lanes are restricted to carpools; any driver with at least one passenger qualifies. Speeding and carpool-violation fines cost hundreds of dollars. Watch out for speed traps in residential and school zones, and especially along Hwy 1.

Do not drink (or do drugs) and drive. A blood alcohol concentration of 0.08% or more can result in arrest, jail time, heavy fines and suspension of your license.

DRIVER'S LICENSE & PERMIT

You can drive in LA with a valid driver's license issued in your home country. If your license is not in English, you may be required to show an international driving permit.

Taxi

Taxis aren't flagged down on the street; call for one instead. Try **Yellow Cab** (☎ 800-200-1085). Fares are metered: $2 at flag-fall, then $2 per mile. Beware of costly snarled traffic. Surcharges for airport drop-offs and pick-ups, extra passengers or luggage may apply.

PRACTICALITIES
Climate & When to Go

SoCal is blessed by sunshine and moderate temperatures, and it's a year-round destination. Summer highs are in the mid-80s

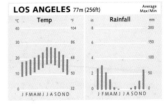

(30°C) to low 90s (33°C) and winter lows are in the mid-50s (13°C) to low 60s (17°C). Peak tourist seasons are summer vacation (late May to early September) and before Christmas through New Year's.

Heavy rains often occur between December and February. Still, the annual average rainfall is under 15in. Drought is an ever-present danger, particularly when Santa Ana winds blow in off the high desert, usually between October and March, sparking wildfires among the chaparral-covered mountains around the LA Basin.

Disabled Travelers
Public buildings, restrooms and transportation (buses, trains and taxis) are required by law to be wheelchair-accessible. Larger hotels and motels have suites or rooms for disabled guests. Listings in this book that are wheelchair-friendly are indicated by the ♿ icon. Telephone companies are required to provide relay operators for the hearing impaired. Many banks now provide ATM instructions in Braille and you'll find audible crossing signals and dropped curbs at many intersections. Seeing-eye dogs may legally be brought into restaurants, hotels and other businesses.

For paratransit and door-to-door services, contact **Access Services Incorporated** (☎ 800-827-0829). With advance reservations, many car-rental agencies provide hand-controlled vehicles or vans with wheelchair lifts; **Wheelers** (☎ 800-456-1371) specializes in such vehicles. Disabled parking at blue-colored curbs and specially designated spots in public lots is by permit only.

INFORMATION & ORGANIZATIONS
If you need advice or help in LA, contact the **LA County Commission on Disabilities** (☎ 213-974-1053, TTY 213-974-1707). The **Society for Accessible Travel & Hospitality** (SATH; ☎ 212-447-7284; www.sath .org) publishes accessibility guides and *Open World*, a magazine for disabled travelers.

Discounts
For combined admission to some sights, try the Hollywood CityPass (p7). Most attractions in LA admit children up to a certain age for free, or sell kids' tickets at reduced rates; family passes for two adults and two children offer substantial savings. Don't forget to look for discount admission coupons in hotel racks of free tourist brochures.

STUDENT & YOUTH CARDS
An ISIC or university ID card entitles you to discounts on museum admission, theater tickets and some attractions.

SENIORS' CARDS
People over the age of 65 (or sometimes 55) typically qualify for the same discounts as students, and then some. Any photo ID is usually sufficient proof of age.

The **American Association of Retired Persons** (AARP; ☎ 888-687-2277; www .aarp.org; annual membership $12.50) offers comprehensive travel bargains for over-50s.

Electricity
Voltage	110V
Frequency	60Hz
Cycle	AC
Plugs	two flat vertical prongs, some times with a third round ground

Visitors from outside North America should bring a universal adaptor or buy one from a travel specialty shop, often found at airports.

Embassies & Consulates
Australia (☎ 310-229-4800; 19th fl, Century Plaza Towers, 2049 Century Park E, Century City)
Canada (7, B4; ☎ 213-346-2700; 9th fl, 550 S Hope St, downtown LA)
Mexico (☎ 213-351-6800; 2401 W 6th St, MacArthur Park)

New Zealand (3, C3; ☎ 310-566-6555; ste 600E, 2425 Olympic Blvd, Koreatown)
South Africa (5, D5; ☎ 323-651-0902; ste 600, 6300 Wilshire Blvd, Mid-City)
UK (☎ 310-481-0031; ste 1200, 11766 Wilshire Blvd, West LA)

Emergencies

During earthquakes, stand under a sturdy door frame and protect your head with your arms until tremors subside. Road accidents are the greatest single risk of injury in LA. Car theft and car-jackings are more common here than in other parts of the country. There is violent crime, but it is mostly confined to well-defined areas of East LA and South LA, as well as less-trafficked blocks in Hollywood, Venice and downtown LA. Avoid these areas after dark. Downtown is also home to many homeless folks, most of whom gather on 'Skid Row,' an area roughly bounded by 3rd, Alameda, 7th and Main Sts.

Police, fire, ambulance (☎ 911)
Police (non-emergency)
    (☎ 877-275-5273)
Rape Crisis Line (☎ 213-626-3393)
Rape Treatment Center
    (☎ 310-319-4000)

Fitness
GYMS

Most top-end hotels have small fitness centers. Otherwise, gyms all over the city sell day passes (around $25). Try:

Crunch Gym (5, D2; ☎ 323-654-4550; www.crunch.com; 8000 W Sunset Blvd, West Hollywood; ☺ 5am-midnight Mon-Fri, 7am-10pm Sat & Sun) Pioneers new fitness trends.

Gold's Gym (4, A4; ☎ 310-392-6004; www.goldsgym.com; 360 Hampton Dr, Venice; ☺ 4am-midnight Mon-Fri, 5am-11pm Sat & Sun) Near the bodybuilders' mecca of Muscle Beach.

Ketchum YMCA (7, B4; ☎ 213-624-2348; www.ymcala.org; 401 S Hope St, downtown

LA; ☺ 5:30am-11pm Mon-Thu, 5:30am-9pm Fri, 8am-6pm Sat, 11am-6pm Sun) A community gym for both sexes.

RUNNING, CYCLING & IN-LINE SKATING

Rental shops are plentiful in Santa Monica, Venice, Manhattan and Hermosa Beaches, all connected by the 20-mile South Bay Trail, a paved recreational path. Runners and hikers also take to the strenuous slopes of Griffith Park (p12). The **Sierra Club Angeles Chapter** (☎ 213-387-4287; www.angeles.sierraclub.org) offers nature hikes and group outings.

SWIMMING

LA's coastal beaches (p16) offer terrific water sports. Swimming is usually prohibited after major storms, because of pollution run-off. Strong currents (riptides) account for most lifeguard rescues – if caught in one, go with the flow until it loses power, even if it means going further out to sea, or swim parallel to the shore to slip out of it. Most **municipal pools** (☎ 323-906-7953; www.ci.la.ca.us /RAP) charge a nominal fee, are outdoors and open seasonally during summer.

Gay & Lesbian Travelers

Los Angeles is one of the most gay-friendly cities in the USA. West Hollywood (WeHo) is Boystown central, while Silver Lake and North Hollywood cater to both sexes. Santa Monica, Venice and Long Beach have laid-back gay and lesbian communities. For entertainment venues, see p64. The age of consent for homosexual sex is 18 (the same as for heterosexuals).

INFORMATION & ORGANIZATIONS

Fab! (www.gayfab.com) Free biweekly newspaper available in WeHo and other hot spots.

LA Gay & Lesbian Center (5, C1; ☎ 323-993-7400; www.laglc.org; 1625 N Schrader Blvd, Hollywood) A one-stop agency.

Health

Travel insurance is strongly advised to cover any medical treatment you may need while in Los Angeles. Medical care is very expensive, and many doctors and hospitals will insist on payment before treatment. American citizens should check with their insurer about any travel conditions on their policy.

MEDICAL SERVICES

For injuries or illnesses that are non-catastrophic, do not visit hospital emergency rooms. Faster and cheaper are neighborhood 'urgent care' centers and doctors' walk-in clinics.

Hospitals with 24-hour accident and emergency departments include:

Cedars-Sinai Medical Center (5, C4; ☎ 310-423-3277; 8700 Beverly Blvd, Beverly Hills)

Hollywood Presbyterian Medical Center (5, G6; ☎ 213-413-3000; 1300 N Vermont Ave, Los Feliz)

UCLA Medical Center (3, B2; ☎ 310-825-8518; 10833 Le Conte Ave, West LA)

PHARMACIES

Many city branches of chain pharmacies, such as Sav-On, Rite Aid and Walgreens, stay open around the clock.

Holidays

Many public holidays are observed on the following Monday.

New Year's Day January 1
Martin Luther King Jr Day 3rd Monday in January
Presidents' Day 3rd Monday in February
Easter March/April
Memorial Day last Monday of May
Independence Day July 4
Labor Day 1st Monday in September
Columbus Day 2nd Monday in October
Veterans' Day November 11
Thanksgiving 4th Thursday of November
Christmas Day December 25

Imperial System

Temperatures are reported in degrees Fahrenheit, not Celsius. Distances are measured in inches (in), feet (ft), yards (yd) and miles (mi). Dry weights are ounces (oz), pounds (lb) and tons. Gasoline is dispensed by the US gallon, which is nearly 20% less than the imperial gallon; US pints (pt) and quarts (qt) are similarly undersized.

TEMPERATURE

$$°C = (°F - 32) \div 1.8$$
$$°F = (°C \times 1.8) + 32$$

DISTANCE
1in = 2.54cm
1cm = 0.39in
1m = 3.3ft = 1.1yd
1ft = 0.3m
1km = 0.62 miles
1 mile = 1.6km

WEIGHT
1kg = 2.2lb
1lb = 0.45kg
1g = 0.04oz
1oz = 28g

VOLUME
1L = 0.26 US gallons
1 US gallon = 3.8L
1L = 0.22 imperial gallons
1 imperial gallon = 4.55L

Internet

Most hotel and some motel rooms are equipped with data ports; better hotels offer high-speed Internet access. Internet cafés and business centers, such as 24-hour branches of **FedEx Kinko's** (☎ 800-254-6567; www.fedexkinkos.com), are common. Logging on at public libraries is free, but requires signing up in person; some branches now provide free wi-fi for laptop users. Special pay phones at LAX have data ports for laptop Internet connections.

INTERNET SERVICE PROVIDERS

Major ISPs such as **EarthLink** (☎ 888-327-8454; www.earthlink.net) and **AOL** (☎ 800-392-5180; www.aol.com) each have dozens of local dial-up numbers across greater LA.

INTERNET CAFÉS

There are many cybercafés in LA, including:
Cyber Java (5, A1; ☎ 323-466-5600; www.cyberjava.com; 7080 Hollywood Blvd, Hollywood; per hr $6; ☼ 7am-11:30pm)
EZ New Web Laundromat & Cafe (3, C3; ☎ 310-559-3279; 6144 Washington Blvd, Culver City; per 30min $5; ☼ 6am-10pm Mon-Fri, 7am-10pm Sat & Sun)
Interactive Cafe (4, A2; ☎ 310-395-5009; 215 Broadway, Santa Monica; per 10min $1; ☼ 6am-1am Sun-Thu, 6am-2am Fri & Sat)

USEFUL WEBSITES

The **Lonely Planet** website (www.lonely planet.com) offers a speedy link to many LA-related websites. Other good sites include:
www.at-la.com Ultimate Web portal to all things LA.
www.blacknla.com Comprehensive info for African Americans.
www.calendarlive.com Arts and culture from the *Los Angeles Times*.
www.la.com Hip shopping, eating and nightlife guide.
www.latinola.com For Latino arts and entertainment.
www.visitlosangeles.info Official website of the LAVCB (p91).

Money
ATMS

Interbank ATM exchange rates usually beat traveler's checks or exchanging foreign currency. Found everywhere, especially outside banks and at shops, almost all ATMs accept cards from major international networks.

Charges to use ATMs other than your own home bank's average $1 to $2; Washington Mutual ATMs have no surcharges. You can also avoid fees by using your debit card to get cash back at supermarkets and gas stations.

CHANGING MONEY

Banks offer better rates than most bureaux de change. The latter are clustered at LAX and in downtown, Hollywood and Santa Monica. **American Express** (5, D5; ☎ 310-659-1682; 8493 W 3rd St; ☼ 9am-6pm Mon-Fri, 10am-3pm Sat) has a travel office near the Beverly Center. **Thomas Cook** (5, A5; ☎ 310-274-9177; 421 N Rodeo Dr; ☼ 10am-6pm Mon-Fri) has an office in Beverly Hills. Always ask about rates, commissions and any surcharges.

CREDIT CARDS

Visa and MasterCard are widely accepted, American Express (Amex), Discover and JCB less so. Credit cards are often required for car rentals, hotel registration and purchasing advance tickets. For 24-hour card cancellations or assistance, call:
American Express (☎ 800-528-4800)
Discover (☎ 800-347-2683)
JCB (☎ 800-366-4522)
MasterCard (☎ 800-826-2181)
Visa (☎ 800-336-8472)

CURRENCY

US currency (the dollar) is divided into 100 cents (¢). Coins come in 1¢ (penny), 5¢ (nickel), 10¢ (dime), 25¢ (quarter), 50¢ (half-dollar; these are rare) and $1 denominations. Notes come in $1, $2 (also rare), $5, $10, $20, $50 and $100. Gas stations, convenience stores and fast-food eateries may not accept bills over $20.

TRAVELER'S CHECKS

Checks issued by **American Express** (☎ 800-221-7282), **Visa** (☎ 800-227-6811) and **Thomas Cook** (☎ 800-287-7362) are accepted at most businesses and can be replaced if they are lost or stolen. Small shops, markets and fast-food chains may refuse them.

Newspapers & Magazines

The *Los Angeles Times* (www.latimes.com) is a respected daily newspaper. Insider showbiz trade papers such as *Variety* (www.variety .com) and *Hollywood Reporter* (www.holly woodreporter.com) are devoured. Usually available at bookstores, bars and cafés on

Thursday, free *LA Weekly* (www.laweekly .com) covers entertainment and politics. Glossy *Los Angeles Magazine* (www.lamag .com) has an urbane readership. Foreign newspapers are sold at chain bookstores and newsstands.

Opening Hours

Banks (8:30am-4:30pm Mon-Thu, 8:30am-5:30pm Fri, some also open 9am-2pm Sat)
Businesses (9am-5pm Mon-Fri)
Post offices (8:30am-5:30pm Mon-Fri, some also open 8:30am-3:30pm Sat)
Restaurants (lunch 11am-2:30pm; dinner 5:30-9:30pm, later on weekends)
Shops (10am-6pm Mon-Sat, shopping malls may close later, noon-5pm Sun)

It's easy to find 24-hour supermarkets, pharmacies, convenience stores, gas stations and diners.

Banks, schools and government offices (including post offices) are closed on major holidays (p88), when public transit, museums and other services use a Sunday schedule. Businesses may close on July 4, Thanksgiving, Christmas Day and New Year's Day.

Post

The **US Postal Service** (USPS; ☎ 800-275-8777, TDD/TTY 877-877-7833; www.usps .gov) is inexpensive. Call the toll-free number for the nearest branch location; most have after-hours stamp vending machines. You can also buy stamps (usually for more than face value) from hotel concierges, convenience stores and supermarkets.

POSTAL RATES

Destination	Postcard	1oz Letter
USA	23¢	37¢
Canada & Mexico	50¢	60¢
Other International	70¢	80¢

Telephone

Public payphones are either coin- or card-operated; some also accept credit cards. Local calls usually cost 35¢ minimum.

PHONECARDS

Private prepaid phonecards are available at newsstands, convenience stores, supermarkets and pharmacies. Cards advertising the cheapest per-minute rates may charge hefty connection fees for each call (especially from pay phones). Cards sold by major telecommunications companies like AT&T may offer better deals and service.

CELL PHONES

The USA uses a variety of cell phone systems, most of which are incompatible with the GSM 900/1800 standard used in Europe, Asia and Africa. To avoid exorbitant roaming surcharges, check with your cellular service provider before departure about using your phone in LA. Mobile phone rentals are available at the airport (p83). Deluxe hotels may also rent or provide cell phones for guests.

COUNTRY & CITY CODES

LA County is divided into several area codes. There is no need to dial the area code to make a local call. Always dial '1' before toll-free (800, 888 etc) numbers. International rates apply for calls to Canada, even though the dialing code (☎ 1) is the same as for US long-distance calls.

Anaheim (☎ 714)
Beverly Hills, Santa Monica, South Bay & Malibu (☎ 310)
Burbank & San Fernando Valley (☎ 818)
Downtown LA (☎ 213)
Hollywood, Los Feliz, Silver Lake & Mid-City (☎ 323)
Pasadena & San Gabriel Valley (☎ 626)
USA (☎ 1)

USEFUL PHONE NUMBERS

Collect (reverse-charge) (☎ 0)
International direct dial code (☎ 011)
International operator (☎ 00)
Local directory inquiries (☎ 411)
Time (☎ 853-1212)

Toll-free directory inquiries
(☎ 800-555-1212)
Weather (☎ 213-554-1212)

Time

Pacific Standard Time (PST) is eight hours behind GMT/UTC. During Daylight Saving Time (first Sunday in April to last Saturday in October), the clock moves ahead one hour.

At noon in Los Angeles it's:

3pm in New York
8pm in London
9pm in Johannesburg
6am (next day) in Sydney
8am (next day) in Auckland

Tipping

Tip restaurant servers 15% to 20%, except for outrageously rude service. If the restaurant automatically adds a 'service charge' (usually 18% for groups of six or more), do not double-tip. Bartenders get at least $1 for one or two drinks, 15% when buying a round. Tip taxi drivers 10% of the fare, rounding up to the nearest dollar. Valet parking attendants get $2 when they hand you back the keys to your car. Skycaps, bellhops and cloak room attendants get $1 to $2 per item; housekeepers are tipped $1 to $2 per day. Concierges receive up to $20 for hard-to-get tickets and restaurant tables.

Tourist Information

The **Los Angeles Convention and Visitors Bureau** (LACVB; www.lacvb.com) provides city maps, brochures and lodging information, plus tickets to theme parks and other attractions, at:

Downtown Los Angeles Visitor Information Center (7, A4; ☎ 213-689-8822; 685 S Figueroa St, downtown LA; ☷ 9am-5pm Mon-Fri)

Hollywood Visitor Information Center (5, B1; ☎ 323-467-6412; Hollywood & Highland, 6801 Hollywood Blvd, Hollywood; ☷ 10am-10pm Mon-Sat, 10am-7pm Sun)

Other useful tourist offices include:

Beverly Hills Conference & Visitors Bureau (5, B5; ☎ 310-248-1015, 800-345-2210; www.beverlyhillsbehere.com; 239 S Beverly Dr, Beverly Hills; ☷ 8:30am-5pm Mon-Fri)

California Welcome Center (5, C4; ☎ 310-854-7616; Beverly Center, 8500 Beverly Blvd, Mid-City; ☷ 10am-6pm Mon-Sat, 11am-6pm Sun)

Pasadena Convention & Visitors Bureau (1, C2; ☎ 626-795-9311, 800-307-7977; www.pasadenacal.com; 171 S Los Robles Ave, Pasadena; ☷ 8am-5pm Mon-Fri, 10am-4pm Sat)

Santa Monica Visitors Center (4, A2; ☎ 310-319-6263, 800-544-5319; www.santamonica.com; 1920 Main St, Santa Monica; ☷ 9am-6pm)

Santa Monica Visitors Kiosk (4, A2; Palisades Park, 1400 Ocean Ave, Santa Monica; ☷ 10am-4pm Sep-May, 10am-5pm Jun-Aug)

Index

See also separate indexes for Eating (p94), Entertainment (p94), Shopping (p94), Sleeping (p95) and Sights with map references (p95).

FEATURES

Moonshadows	*Eating*
Zanzibar	*Entertainment*
Tiki Ti	*Drinking*
Universal Studios	*Highlights*
Moondance	*Shopping*
Getty Center	*Sights/Activities*
Georgian Hotel	*Sleeping*
	Beach

AREAS

	Beach, Desert
	Building
	Land
	Mall
	Other Area
	Park/Cemetery
	Sports
	Urban

HYDROGRAPHY

	River, Creek
	Intermittent River
	Canal
	Swamp
	Water

BOUNDARIES

	State, Provincial
	Regional, Suburb
	Ancient Wall

ROUTES

	Tollway
	Freeway
	Primary Road
	Secondary Road
	Tertiary Road
	Lane
	Under Construction
	One-Way Street
	Unsealed Road
	Mall/Steps
	Tunnel
	Walking Path
	Walking Trail/Track
	Pedestrian Overpass
	Walking Tour

TRANSPORT

	Airport, Airfield
	Bus Route
	Cycling, Bicycle Path
	Ferry
	General Transport
	Metro
	Monorail
	Rail
	Taxi Rank
	Tram

SYMBOLS

	Bank, ATM
	Buddhist
	Castle, Fortress
	Christian
	Diving, Snorkeling
	Embassy, Consulate
	Hospital, Clinic
	Information
	Internet Access
	Islamic
	Jewish
	Lighthouse
	Lookout
	Monument
	Mountain, Volcano
	National Park
	Parking Area
	Petrol Station
	Picnic Area
	Point of Interest
	Police Station
	Post Office
	Ruin
	Telephone
	Toilets
	Zoo, Bird Sanctuary
	Waterfall